Tony Hill

Tony Hill hails from Jacksdale: an old mining village on the Nottinghamshire/Derbyshire border, deep in D.H. Lawrence country. The world famous writer used to come dancing in Tony's village; where he had a great time, until, allegedly, getting knocked out for not supporting a local team. This is mentioned in Tony's books *If the Kids are United* and *The Palace and the Punks*. One of the last authors to be published by Victor Gollancz (before the Orion takeover), his - *Kes* evoking - book *If the Kids are United* was called 'the working-class *Fever Pitch*,' and received 5 and 4 star reviews.

www.manutdbooks.com

Also by Tony Hill
If the Kids are United

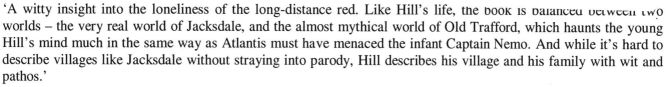

'A witty insight into the loneliness of the long-distance red. Like Hill's life, the book is balanced between two worlds – the very real world of Jacksdale, and the almost mythical world of Old Trafford, which haunts the young Hill's mind much in the same way as Atlantis must have menaced the infant Captain Nemo. And while it's hard to describe villages like Jacksdale without straying into parody, Hill describes his village and his family with wit and pathos.'
★★★★★ *Four Four Two*

'This story of a Red growing up in a pit village during the 70's and 80's is both funny and sad at times...a great read.'
4/5 Glory Glory Man United (MUFC official magazine)

'For younger fans, there is an intoxicating account of the run-in to Fergie's first title triumph in 1993, while older fans will relish exhilarating memories of United in the 70's, a decade of Cup finals and cock-ups. Equally entertaining is Hill's witty and often poignant portrayal of a youth spent in a declining mining community...Impassioned and bleak but also hilarious.'
Manchester UNITED (the official MUFC magazine)

'Hill can be funny, but really finds his voice in harrowing recollections of the Hillsborough tragedy.'
Daily Mail

'A laddish feast of music, football and autobiography. Hill's passion for the game shines out like floodlights at a night-time match.'
Nottingham Evening Post

'Tony Hill made his momentous decision to become a Red Devils supporter in the 1970's and for the next twenty-two years lived and breathed to bag a Cup Final ticket. In this hilarious debut, Hill describes his consistently thwarted attempts to get his hands on the elusive voucher.'
EGO

'A days-of-our-lives view of Man United from the wilderness years of the 70's to the rattling rise of Fergie's Red army.'
★★★★ *Total Football*

'An East Midlands Fever Pitch without the middle-class guilt complex. It also points out that D.H. Lawrence got panned in a local pub for not supporting a Nottingham team.'
Left Lion

The Palace and the Punks

'It was as likely as finding a diamond in your dustbin. There it was in the heart of a scruffy, coal-scarred mining village whose narrow, terraced streets had no-nonsense names like Edward and Albert. Inside an old converted cinema, beneath a nicotine-stained ceiling, a local entrepreneur named Alf Hyslop opened a music venue called the Grey Topper. Somehow this nondescript, unvarnished venue managed to become part of music history. Tony Hill's book is a must-read for any muso who boogied, rocked or pogo-ed at anytime from '69 to '81.'
Nottingham Evening Post

'A very good and interesting perspective of those times.'
Andy Scott, Glam Rock band Sweet

'You can see the sweat dripping off the ceiling, sense the globule of spit skimming past your cheek, feel the poke in the eye of a spiky mohican or hear the rattling of bondage straps on pogoing punks. Tony Hill's book paints such a vivid picture of the Grey Topper that you're in there, sharing the hopes of the bands on the threshold of stardom or the despair of those on their way down. A compelling read.'
Derbyshire Times

'Endlessly gobsmacking...piss yourself laughing...like music books? Buy this.'
Left Lion magazine

'Highly recommended, very entertaining.'
Pete Davies, drummer UK Subs

'A great little piece of highly personal, social history of which we should see more. I would recommend it very highly to anyone with a passing interest in the history of the late 70's UK punk scene.'
Aural Sculptors

If the Kids are United
The Palace and the Punks
Skye-Walker's Landscapes of Legends Quest
The Curse of the Crooked Spire and other fairytales
The Glastonbury Spirit and other tales of the supernatural
The Flowers of Romance
Glastonbury Tour
www.manutdbooks.com

EVEN EVEREST SHOOK
CAUGHT IN THE NEPAL EARTHQUAKE 2015

Tony Hill

Northern Lights Lit

Even Everest Shook
Caught in the Nepal Earthquake 2015

Enormous, ominous, storm clouds billowed up and up into the heavens, illuminated by lightning forks from hell below. There were gasps around the cabin as the airplane entered into this turbulent atmosphere, giving us an extreme theme park Drop Tower experience, stomachs in mouth. Windows in the clouds gave a glimpse of the valley rising up ever nearer, the northern sprawl of Kathmandu spreading up into the hills, communities whose houses seem to perch precariously on the steep valley sides.

This wasn't the welcome to Nepal I was expecting. All posts on TripAdvisor, all I'd read online, told of very little rainfall and mostly clear skies in April, the latter the most important to me as my ultimate goal on the trip was to reach Everest Base Camp and be rewarded with a view of the mightiest mountain of legend. The skies in October are clearer but I chose spring for my trek as the lower valleys would be Mother Nature decorated with rhododendrons (the national flower of Nepal) this appealed to me, as simple as that.

Why choose to walk to see Everest in the first place? A few days before, driving up to Manchester (where I would leave my car at my sister's in Chorlton to catch the flight from the city's airport the next day), my iPod - connected to the car stereo, on shuffle - had thrown up the track 'The Race for Space' by Public Service Broadcasting, samples of the haunting and powerful voice of JFK, giving the reasons for choosing to go to the moon: 'many years ago, the great British explorer George Mallory, who was to die on Mount Everest, was asked why he wanted to climb it "because it is there"....space is there and we're going to climb it, the moon is there and the planets'....A great, succinct, stiff upper lip British Empire reply. But I'm sure when/if Mallory opened up his soul, he would talk for hours with power and emotion about his real reasons to put his life on the line attempting to scale Everest: he was already a great mountaineer, Everest established as the highest peak in the world, the overwhelming lure to put his skill, courage, bravery and endurance to the test and conquer it, be the first to do so, for the glory of Britain. It must have run as deep as the Himalayan valleys within him, become an obsession.

In a run of Everest and Himalayan coincidences, BBC 4 had shown a series of programmes on the subject just a few days after I'd booked the trip, 'The Battle for the Himalayas' and the official 1920's film of Mallory's expedition to Everest. The latter like a flick book of old black and white photo album images. Until the cameraman could travel with them no closer to Everest, his iconic views of the mountain and the advance of the expedition captured through an ingenious early type of telescopic lens. That haunting last shot of Mallory and Irvine; moving dots, ants, crawling along the shoulder of the giant queen of mountains, to be seen alive no more (Mallory's body was discovered in 1999). The search parties setting off days later, the round window zooming in on their return in the distance, to see them making the shape of a cross in the snow to signal 'all hope is lost.'

Milton Keynes is there, the Tory Party Conference is there, Wormwood Scrubs is there, but I've no desire to go to any of them just because they are there. I didn't want to go to Everest just because I'd seen a picture of it in a magazine and thought it would be a fun to go there. I love walking, nature, the breathtaking scenery of mountainous landscapes, places on earth of power, beauty and majesty that make humans insignificant little clusters of space dust blowing around on their surface.

I love human history, culture and achievements too. So all in all, spending a few days in Kathmandu, visiting the ancient squares, Hindu and Buddhist temples and shrines and statues, and holy people, before trekking up through the Himalayan valleys to Everest Base Camp, seemed like the ultimate adventure to me. In the top 5 in my bucket list, and with my body starting to pick up persistent injuries in the previous 18 months – a back injury, pains seemingly in every muscle in my flat feet after long walks, a torn knee ligament that was taking an age to fully heal – as I get nearer to being 50, I decided it was now or possibly never to live this dream.

Ironically I didn't know that mere mortals like myself could get anywhere near Mt Everest (other than flying over it) until watching and reading news reports of the catastrophic avalanche of April 2014, the worst disaster in Everest's history, claiming 16 lives, and the Base Camp trek was mentioned. So, I thought, there is a non climbing walk I could possibly do, through the majestic Himalayan Mountains, giving a view of Everest? Even the Annapurna Circuit snow storm disaster in October 2014, when over 40 people were killed, including many trekkers, didn't deter me. Paradoxically I was even more attracted to the Himalayan walks as I checked them out online, then sort of filed it away at the back of my mind to maybe, just maybe, go and do one day.

I can't really put my finger on precisely why I suddenly went ahead and booked it this year, one of those spontaneous decisions in my life, sparked by a combination of factors I guess. An old friend called Kevin from my teenage punk years, who loved walking, nature and adventure, loved life, more than most, until tragically breaking his back and becoming paralysed from the chest down after falling from a tree in his 20's. He lived on, always in the hope a scientific breakthrough would come along enabling him to walk, to run again. 20 years passed before he committed suicide in 2014. Kevin was certainly on my mind when I booked a hiking holiday in Scotland in the spring of that year and Everest in 2015. He'd be shouting out for me to get off my arse and do such things he could only dream of, and I was very capable and lucky to do.

Then there was the Facebook profiles of my friends, so many had travelled; like my beautiful friend Siobhan, who'd spent 9 months travelling around the world with her boyfriend, musician Zackie Chan, the trip of a lifetime that I couldn't hear enough about when we met up. One set of their travel pictures in particular making me green with envy, those showing the Machhapuchchhre 'fish tail' mountain in the Himalayas, even in photographs it looked an awe inspiring sight.

The loss of people in my life in recent years, dad from cancer, Kev as mentioned, a friend in a motorbike accident, my sister's best friend Alison to cancer in her 30's, my body starting to show signs of wear and tear, the realisation that we're all walking sand timers, the grains of life dropping off of us every moment of every day. I was content with the life I'd had, seeing much of the best of what Britain had to offer, in scenery, history, culture, music and football, getting published about my UK experiences in the latter two. Yet the only travel abroad I'd done was two trips to the Ostend beer festival when in my 20's, and those are just a drunken blur. Real travel was a big void in my life, I needed to experience the bigger picture, broaden my mind. So in January I made the quick fire decision, Everest Base Camp in April, and when I make up my mind about something nothing will stop me, I fully commit.

*

I usually give up drinking after Christmas for several weeks, and after booking the Everest trek I made the decision to quit entirely (well save for a spoonful of brandy and the odd tipple at night to keep out the chills of an English winter), until I'd achieved my objective. The prize would be pints back in my local pub in May after hopefully making it to Everest Base Camp.

My Everest or bust fitness regime had begun, not that I looked the part: old Compo woolly hat, ripped and patched up (many times) jeans, worn out hiking boots with splits and holes that let in water, stubble on my chin, eyes still bloodshot from the Christmas overindulgence sessions, and half limping as a result of slipping in the snow and ice on New Year's Eve, worsening my ligament torn, damaged right knee. Shuffling along in this state in the winter rain and snow of January I looked more like 'Ratso' in *Midnight Cowboy* than an Intrepid Everest explorer. My border collie dog, Flossy, joined me of my fitness walks, and didn't seem to mind at all, in fact enjoyed the extra hours of walks. Until I started running up that hill, a cardiovascular short sharp shock of a hill, up to the ruins of an old castle; this situated above my old coal mining village of Jacksdale, on the Nottinghamshire/ Derbyshire border.

On my first attempt I failed miserably. Attempt 2 (with Placebo's cover of Kate Bush's 'Running Up That Hill' motivating me on my iPod) I made it all the way up but it nearly killed me, my heart pumping so hard it felt like it would burst out of my chest, gasping for breath for minutes after, feeling sick. Flossy just looked confused, but barely panted and wagged her tail in anticipation of the chewy stick treat she would receive, whilst I knocked back a flask containing a combination of fruit juices, barley water, lemonade with a drop or two of brandy and a cereal energy bar to eat.

Thereafter I could run up that hill (and other steep ones in the area) with no problem. Although it never really became any easier after a certain level, my breathing improved and recovered quicker. Towards mid March I was at last beginning to feel I was reaching the level of fitness I felt I needed to be in to give myself a good chance of completing the Everest Base Camp trek. It was still, however, a bit of a balancing act trying not to further injure my back, feet and knee (plenty of yoga, Epsom Salt body and feet baths, aromatherapy oils, Ibuprofen and prayers to my personal angels and protectors). I looked more the part, new hiking gear, boots and a water and windproof jacket. I even purchased a pair of Bear Grylls hiking trousers, but was thankful there were just his initials BG in orange on the trousers and not his full name as I would have felt a delusional adventurer idiot otherwise.

Gradually I was buying in - from the likes of Decathlon and Amazon - all the gear I would need, along with water purification tablets and travel medicines; I visited the doctors for the essential travel vaccinations. But after having the first of the optional rabies jabs and being charged over £40 - and that was just for the first of 3 - I didn't go back for the last 2, deciding to take my chances against getting bit by anything rabid. I was looking forward to seeing monkeys up at the Swayambhunath 'monkey temple,' but would keep a distance from them. As for dogs, I guessed there'd be a few strays around…turned out they ran wild, ran free everywhere, loads of them with their own society and pecking order going on, the lady and several hundred tramp dogs.

I'd read blogs and tips from people who'd done the Everest Base Camp trek, made notes of - and printed out - all the vital information and 'places to see' on TripAdvisor. Then I read up on Nepalese culture and history and brought my palms together to practice 'Namaste' in the mirror. I learned, not for the first time in my life, that being left handed made me potentially evil and try and remember not to use it, and showing the souls of my feet is rude.

I gained further knowledge of how the Himalayas were created: India an island some 70 millions years ago, gradually drifting north until the tectonic plate it sat on collided with the Eurasian plate, causing the earth to crumple up and form the Himalayas. The Indian plate continues to push north and under the northern continent, the mighty mountains continue to grow and form a giant wall that Nepal is being pushing into; millions of years from now Nepal will crumble and sink into extinction.

The never ending collision of these plates 'make this region seismically active, leading to earthquakes from time to time.'

I gave little thought to the last sentence; I couldn't ever remember hearing of a major earthquake in Nepal.

With a week to go to my flight out of Manchester to Kathmandu I felt (bearable twinges and aches aside) that I was as fit and prepared as I possibly could be to take on my own personal Everest challenge and adventure. I did one last real long march and run up that bloody castle hill and worked out using the home gym in my spare room. Maybe I was feeling too cocky about the level of fitness I'd attained through hard work?.....It was just a box of books that needed moving upstairs into the spare room, but without correctly adopting the lifting stance - i.e. straightening my back whilst bending my knees - I just yanked the box off the ground and up…and, felt my back go. A sharp, deep pain like someone was constantly kneeling into the lower left of my spine, with spasms of pain shooting up and down my leg. I called my self a f#~**%n idiot and swore too at Mr Sod and his law. For several agonising hours, mentally and physically, I wondered if my dream trip was over before it had begun.

The pain was there constantly, when sitting or lying down or even having a bath. The great relief was next day when I found that the pain actually went away when walking. This I did gingerly at first, then thought fuck it, throw the dice, go for it and started marching fast, then burst into a small run up a hill, and my back felt fine. Phew, I just prayed that it didn't give way hugging my heavy luggage through the airports on route, and that the steep climbs up into the Himalayas would strengthen and not further strain my back (and by then we would have Sherpas to carry our heavy bags). All systems go again.

Diary entry:
Sat Apr 18th 2015
Everest Base Camp was on breakfast news this morning, as it was a year ago today: one of the worst ever avalanches occurred in the area, taking the lives of 16 people (the worst ever mass loss of life there), mainly Sherpas died. Today all trekking, climbs and preparation for the conquest of Everest came to a standstill for respect and prayers to be given for the lost.

Hope mum didn't see it, she's already worried I could be kidnapped by Isis in the Middle East (if I left Doha airport), or convert to Buddhism (wouldn't that be a good thing?) and not come back. Or crash in an aircraft, or be mugged, or bitten by a snake or rabid monkey or dog, without throwing in the risk of being swallowed by an avalanche.

There looked to be plenty of snow at EBC, excited now, the big pack tomorrow.

On Monday April 20th, bags packed, I posted a message on Facebook:
Off Yeti hunting*

"Down below, emerging from an igloo,
intrigued by the Wizard wagon hullabaloo,
but with white fluffy ruff unruffled,
giving a long yawn, came a large Yogi Yeti,
carrying a frozen water lily down to a jetty,
to sit upon in a lotus position,
and spin slowly around an ice rink,
to contemplate, meditate and think,
none could start the day calmer,
then write up the inner most findings
for its column in the Yeti newspaper, the Daily Lama."
*enjoy the General Muppet Election.

The poem from a story about a travelling wizard in my book of fairytales, *The Curse of the Crooked Spire*, written long before I'd thought of going to the Himalayas. Yeti Airlines here I come.

On late night TV a few weeks before had been an old Hammer Horror film, *The Abominable Snowman*, quite atmospheric, even if the Yeti's looked silly in the end.

I piled everything into my car, and set off Manchester bound on a beautiful sunny, English spring day; The Jesus and Mary Chain's 'April Skies' coming out of my stereo. As ever in April, though, on passing the signs for Sheffield, my mind briefly turned to the Hillsborough disaster. Mornings like this around the 15th always remind me of the glorious spring weather on the morning of April 15th 1989, when I set off - with friends - in high spirits to go to a football match, and witnessed a great tragedy instead. But I came back and 96 Liverpool fans never did. That day has never left my thoughts, particularly, even after all these years on, the reasons why the disaster occurred have still not been resolved; a new inquiry is going on. They'd spoken to me on the phone in 2014, as my view of the disaster from another angle was a major chapter in my book *If the Kids are United*.

I always tread warily in April: aged 16 in this month, Easter, I'd wheelied a motorbike through a hedge, badly breaking my wrist and cutting up my face; as mentioned I was at the Hillsborough Disaster on the 15th; my dad had died of cancer on the 10th. Yet despite all these calamitous events in April it's a time of year I still look forward to: the end of winter, new life, new start, England looking its best, if the sun shines.

Driving over the top of the Peak District, seeing everything gone green, I felt a great sense of optimism, of freedom, leaving it all behind, flying off on an adventure, eagle's wings bursting out of my back, soaring higher and away. I was hoping to glimpse a golden eagle in the Himalayas. A year before I'd been up in their hunting grounds on the Isle of Skye in Scotland, but never caught sight of one. Maybe I would get lucky this time with those, if the Yeti failed put in an appearance.

On arriving at the home of my sister, Elaine, we had a catch up chat, then a stroll around Chorlton Green and the Mersey Valley, before sitting on a bench in the sun. Back at her flat later, around 6.30pm, she was cooking me a meal, whilst I was going over the Intrepid (my travel company) trip notes, but it still didn't click. A voice came into my head, isn't the flight Monday, tonight? I flicked through the holiday printouts to find the flight information. Oh fuck, because of the distance and connection, changing in Doha, Qatar, the flight was spread over 2 days. I'd been glancing down at the second leg, Tuesday and had it in my head this was the day of the flight out of Manchester. But no, it was this night at 8.00pm!

I shouted out to Elaine in panic for her local taxi number. 'Oh Tony,' she said in exasperation, then sympathy. After all this preparation how could I make such a simple but costly mistake? I could almost cry at the thought of missing the flight and not getting another in time to make the start of the trek. IDIOT!

Luckily the taxi was there within minutes and the last of the rush hour traffic had eased off. The driver dropped me at terminal 2 and I ran inside. The guy at check-in was a star worker, listening to my predicament, promptly checking me in, and then on spotting me at the back of a long queue to hand over my cabin luggage, walking over, picking up my rucksack and taking me to the front of the queue. Because of his thoughtful actions I made it through security and to the departure lounge with just a few minutes to spare to boarding. I sent a text to my sister to let her know, wiped the sweat from my brow, sighed with relief that I hadn't strained my back again and was welcomed with a smile by a beautiful stewardess onto Qatar airlines.

Yes I did have a tipple of whisky to relax me and help me sleep on the overnight flight; this I failed to do as the adrenalin was already pumping. Instead, as I had a window seat, I looked down at the night-time landscape below: the towns, villages and cities of France, the flames of oil refineries in the Middle East. Then I decided to watch an in-flight movie to pass time *The Hobbit: An Unexpected Journey*. I felt like a hobbit (alas my dark curly hair has disappeared, but ever more hair grows on my feet), rarely leaving my shire, but when I do it often turns out to be a great and memorable adventure. The film did drag, though: by the time Bilbo and the dwarfs finally encountered Smaug the dragon, the rest of the passengers in the cabin were awaking from slumber and the sun was rising over Qatar as the plane descended to Doha; its rich gleaming towers shimmering in the morning sun below, in the middle of a desert.

Doha airport is vast, modern, streamlined and very efficient in the ease at which you pass through all the necessary arrival checks. And the enormous halls reflect the wealth of oil rich Qatar: you have the money and want to buy expensive watches, clothes or even a McLaren sports car on route or arrival? Then they are all here. I couldn't even afford the raffle tickets on offer to win the McLaren. I can afford one luxury only, food, junk food at that, I head for Burger King at the end of the food hall, and have a

Steakhouse sandwich and fries – washed down with coke – to stuff my arteries with before going vegetarian in Nepal for few weeks.

It's a 7 hour flight from Doha to Kathmandu, and again I'm lucky to have a window seat to enjoy the views in the early morning light. At Christmas I'd been given a great present, a book by astronaut Chris Hadfield (the one made famous after his rendition of David Bowie's 'Space Oddity' on board the International Space Station went viral online), *You Are Here – Around the World in 92 Minutes* (photos from the ISS), stunning. Like summiting Everest, I was never going to get that far up above the world, but the views from thousands of feet up, cruising over the Middle East, then India from Qatar airlines flight X674F3 were pretty special too. First hugging the coast line, a turquoise sea, white desert islands, oil terminals - one so large with so many oil tankers waiting to fill up that it resembled D Day. Then over southern Iran, a bleached wilderness that stretched on seemingly forever, with just the odd isolated community occasionally visible. A dusty dirt road coming over a desert ridge to a village, not passing through, it ended there, and I'm imagining an old community straight out of *Lawrence of Arabia*. Then over northern India, looking parched too – but a lot more populated – until the monsoon rains come. As in Nepal this shouldn't have been until well into June. Yet as we approached Kathmandu we were in a storm cloud.....

Tuesday April 21st 2015, Kathmandu, Nepal:
....I sighed with relief when the airplane emerged out of monster cumulonimbus, into clearer skies and touched down safely on the runway of Kathmandu International Airport.

I'd read about the chaos of this place and within minutes I'm thrown into it: the scramble for your luggage, snatching at piles of entry visa forms and racing to the arrivals desk. The staff there greet customers to their country with a mixture of indifference, suspicion or scorn. At times they seemingly go off to chat with a work colleague, not about work but to catch up with events over the weekend and show each other photos on their mobiles. When it's my time, the woman scrutinizes my face, my passport is nearly 10 years old, I still had a mop of curly hair then and boyish looks intact, now I have a shaven head on my visa pics and look like Magwitch from *Great Expectations*, and even more tired and rough looking in reality, I'd guess, after the long haul, sleepless flight. And she wants to know why the passport is empty.

'Well I've only flown to Edinburgh since I've had it,' I explain.

'Where Edinburgh, I see no stamp?'

'Scotland, above England, you didn't need one.'

She scowls and carries on checking the passport. 'Nearly run out, you need 8 months on it,' she says shaking her head.

I'm getting worried now, she seems to be getting into a mission to find a way to keep me out. 'It has more than 8 months left on it, take a closer look, it doesn't run out until May 2016.'

She calls over a colleague, he shows her a photo on his mobile, they laugh and have a little chat and finally return to the matter in hand, a nod of heads, my visa is stamped and I'm through and into Nepal.

11

A man with a luggage trolley tries to grab my rucksack, I've read about these too, they'll want paying for wheeling your bags a few yards, I yank it back and indicate I'm fine to carry it myself. More chaos outside the airport - instead of seeing one lone man with a big card with my name on it I'm confronted by a shouting mob of Nepalese, with 3 dozen cards being flashed about and more independent taxi drivers vying for your fare. At last I find a man with an Intrepid card and introduce myself.

'Ah Tom,' he says.

'Er no Tony,' I reply thinking he's just pronounced my name wrong.

He checks a list he's holding, then looks up at me with a puzzled expression, 'Tom?'

'No. Tony, Tony Hill, Tony Richard Hill it may say.'

'Not Tom?'

'No.'

A big white man appears at my side. 'Tom did you say?' he says in a gentle Irish accent.

The man nods.

'I'm Tom.'

The man smiles and ticks Tom off his list. One of the 3 men in the group grabs his bag and starts heading for a taxi.

'Er what about me, I'm booked with Intrepid too,' I butt in and show him my print out.

He inspects this, then his list again, shakes his head, then makes a call on his mobile. And finally nods and smiles at me in an encouraging way. 'Ah Tony Hill, come,' he says heading for a taxi.

One of the other two men grabs my rucksack, walks all of 10 yards and places it in the back of the taxi, as I climb in he says: 'Tip, dollars.'

I'd read on the Intrepid trip notes and on TripAdvisor to tip around $2, and this would seem an adequate amount in my mind, seeing as he's only carried it a very little distance. I open up my wallet, as I do he spots a $10 dollar note.

'Ah ten dollar, give me that,' he says and snatches it out, a big smile on his face. 'Namaste.'

Tom gives them no tip, telling them he's not yet had time to get any cash sorted. Turns out Tom is an experienced traveller, whilst I'll continue to have a big innocent/idiot abroad sign above my head.

Tom and me shake hands and make our introductions. He's a big, softly spoken, easy going, Irishman from Cork, with hints of a dry sense of humour. I like him immediately and feel a sense of relief, well here's one of the group of 16 that I'm sure I'll get on with at least. When looking at Intrepid's 'trip notes' for the Everest trek I'd read about an app you could download to get in touch with the rest of the group before the trip. However, being a bit of a Luddite I don't have a modern multi-tech-tasking-app smartphone, or laptop, I only have a dodgy old PC. So now I'm paranoid that the other 15 will all be tech savvy and have all latest gadgets and gizmos (and all be young!) and will already have downloaded the get to know you app. They'll already be on first name terms, virtual friends, know where each other lives and what their interests are. Will have all been discussing who the mysterious missing number 16 of the party is, as will be the case when we all meet up in person; they'll be shaking hands, and hugging 'how's that project going we chatted about online?' Etc, then a hush will fall as the only stranger, me, walks in.

Soon our attention is drawn to the scenes outside the half opened taxi windows. The first thing that hits you it is that there is no doubt Nepal is a third world country: the poorest of this city, in the outskirts, sit clustered by hovels, on rubbish and rubble strewn wasteland between tumbledown buildings. Roads full of potholes, nothing you could really call a highway and definitely no code for one; our taxi driver pips his horn every few seconds as he weaves his vehicle around other horn pipping vehicles (mainly motorcycles), on both overtaking and avoiding a head on collision, as the few centre lines on the road seem to mean little. He pips too so not to knock down fellow citizens, or stray dogs who wander across the roads seemingly without a care. Many drivers and people walking by are wearing facemasks, and we soon have to wind up the windows so as not to choke on the thick polluted smog; the rise of respiratory ailments amongst the city's residents is soaring.

Kathmandu is one of the most polluted cities on Earth, resulting from a number of factors: the population has soared over the last 10 years, now over 1 million, resulting in the number of vehicles on the poor quality roads to triple. The many brick kilns are also major contributors to air pollution in the winter months, then a near permanent grey blanket of smog sits on the city. The geological location of Kathmandu stops the pollution escaping, it sits in a bowl, surrounded by hills, the terrain stops air circulating out and cold air from the high Himalayas floods down into the valleys and is held in place by warmer air above.

More smoke comes drifting up from a handful of cremations taking place down on the banks of a rubbish strewn polluted river; the quality of ground water and surface water in Kathmandu Valley is also worsening.

And yet there is a vibrancy, colour and character to the people that adheres to your heart. As you head into the city centre and see shops of a myriad wares, glimpse temples and stupas, amongst hotels and ancient squares, you feel the heartbeat, sight and sounds of a city rich in culture, spirituality and history.

Our taxi makes its way through the maze of narrow streets in the Thamel district of Kathmandu, add timber beams and you could be in a medieval English town, think the Shambles of York. Eventually we arrive at the grand, old, Kathmandu Guest House. It almost has a colonial feel to it, the hotel forms a quadrangle around a lovely inner garden, with flowers, green well manicured lawns, a little café and bar and Buddha statues; an oasis to escape the chaos of the streets that surround the hotel.

I'm still impressed by the fact - I'd read online, then the hotel website - that The Beatles stayed here. After booking in and being led up to my room I'm given a detour to see 'The Beatles wing;' along the corridor there is a line of framed photographs showing the most famous group in the history of pop music, from mop top Fab Four days to long haired, bearded, meditating, far out tripping Kathmandu hippie kings.

*

I had planned to dump my bags and go back down into the garden to chill out and unwind after the near 24 hours (well if you move the clocks on for time difference) of frantic travel, but that monster cumulonimbus has rolled in to devour Kathmandu; my room is lit up by a lightning bolt, followed by a loud crack then rumble of thunder, rain beats down. So I close the curtains, crash down on my bed for a nap and later shower.

Despite the storm it's still humid, so I put on my cool black and red Manchester United training top, a waterproof jacket on top of this and set off and explore the streets of Thamel in the gathering gloom. I'm an old terrace Stretford Ender, a United sufferer from the pre Fergie glory years, been there, done that, wore many new team shirts and wrote the book (and got it published). But I stopped wearing the shirts many moons back, when all these glory hunters crawled out of the woodwork wearing them (I thought no one else in my village supported United, I never used to see a United shirt). But thought it would be a good idea to wear one for this trip. 1. They're ideal for trekking in when down in the warm climate of the lower valleys and 2. Guessed they would be a good conversation starter with fellow tourists and United supporting Nepalese too.

Diary entry:
Within minutes of starting to wander the narrow streets of Thamel I'm nearly knocked down, injured or killed, by about 4 guys on mopeds…wearing Manchester United shirts! I've made the mistake of running the crazy street gauntlet for the first time at rush hour (and at other times of the day you have to have your wits about you), and make the second mistake of trying to jump out of the way of the masses of motorbikes weaving through the throng. If they pip, then maybe move aside a little but it's not entirely necessary, they'll avoid you skilfully. It's like they've developed a sixth sense, a collective consciousness – bother riders and pedestrians – on how to avoid each other. During my first 15 minutes encountering this madness I'm convinced I'm going to witness a fatal collision or horrific injury of a man, woman, child, dog or chicken, hit by a bike, but I never see this happen. What you definitely don't want to do, like I did the first few times, is throw up your hands in fear, give a little yelp and try to dash or jump out of the way. This causes a multitude of blasting horns as you're throwing out the synchronized, non contact, easy flowing river of man and animals.

I do find a few relatively quieter side streets and as the darkness falls and the mass of neon signs flicker to life I'm reminded of the downtown streets of the city in *Blade Runner*. Something that draws my attention with a mixture of amazement and amusement are the telephone/electrical posts: attached to them, not too securely by the look of things, are big misshapen balls of tangled wires, like spaghetti on top of a fork. I pity the electrical engineers out on a job up these poles. I'm going to take a photo but want to save my camera batteries; I make a mental note to do so on my return to Kathmandu after Everest.*
*Days after the earthquake I'll hear of the horrific consequences of this disorderly and dangerous set up.

Thamel really is a maze, so as I'm feeling tired and scared of getting lost and not finding my way back to the guest house, I try and trace my way back. The dodgy underworld night dealers are out too, I'm twice offered drugs for sale.

Back at the hotel I go for a meal at their outdoor restaurant, adjacent to the oasis garden. Tom turns up to join me. Unsure what to order I follow his well travelled knowledge of food and copy his order of a bowl of rice, veg curry and spicy spinach, with a pot of ginger tea to follow - very nice too. At the bar, waiting to pay my bill, I get talking to this very animated, but very friendly guy from Canada. I'd seen him around earlier and wondered if he would be part of our Intrepid Everest Base Camp group. But it turns out that he and his girlfriend are travelling around Nepal independently. He's quite impressed when I tell him where I'm off too.

'Are you passing Gokyo lake?' he asks.

I'm not sure we are, but it sounds wonderful what he tells me about it: 'a brilliant blue lake in the heart of the giant Himalayan Mountains.'

Then I'm dismayed to be told by him that they're predicting lousy weather, rain and cloud, for the next 8 days in this area of Nepal. I'm hoping it will be clearer further up the valleys near Everest. We wish each other wonderful travels and go our separate ways.

I'm really feeling jet lagged now and head up to bed, it's only 7.50 pm, but I do manage to drop off to sleep. Not for long, just a few hours, around 9.50 pm I'm woken by brilliant white light and booms of another thunder storm. When this passes, it's the pigeons roosting noisily outside of my room that keep me awake. I can't believe it, in the attic of my home back in England pigeons roost noisily, catching the rod of an old aerial when panicking at the sound of crows on the park out back, and keep me awake. Bloody pigeons, they follow me everywhere: when I was a kid growing up in my Nottinghamshire mining village both flat capped old miners, who lived either side of us, had pigeon lofts. I do manage to grab a few more hours sleep, about 4 in a row, this will be as much as I get in one go for the rest of my time in Nepal.

Wednesday April 22nd 2015, Kathmandu:

At least the sun is shining from clear blue skies when I go down for breakfast next morning. I'm less adventurous in terms of my diet this morning and just fill up my plate and dishes with the offerings from the western style continental breakfast buffet. I do feel refreshed now, energy returning, and as the meeting with the rest of the Intrepid group and trek leader isn't until 2.30 pm I head off out of the hotel to explore.

Part of me wonders if I should put off seeing some of the main Kathmandu hotspots until our return from Everest on May 5th. But I know Durbar Square is nearby and can't resist strolling on down there. A few rickshaw owners seem to guess where I want to go and offer to take me there. I decline, happy to wander the streets, but again I'm getting lost in the maze. Even though I've asked a few western tourists the way, I seem to be getting nowhere nearer and go around in a square circles back to where I'd already passed. So when another rickshaw pulls up and says 'Durbar Square,' I'm ready to jump aboard.

First to negotiate a price. 'How much?' I ask, trying to look and sound the seasoned Englishman abroad.

'Three hundred rupees,' I'm sure he says.

That's reasonable. 'Ok,' I reply jumping up into the seat.

Off he cycles. Before we get to the large and famous Durbar Square he suggests I go see a little old square, tucked away down a side street. I agree, jump down and follow him into there. It is delightful, two bronze lions guard the entrance to the square and on passing them you come into a compact area of temples, shrines, prayer wheels and statues. The centrepiece is gold topped stupa. We slowly circumambulate this.

15

Stupas often have a domed shaped base that represent the body of an enlightened being, inside are Buddhist relics. A cone or spire sits on top; many in Nepal have the eyes of Buddha on the four sides of the square-shaped tower to symbolize his all seeing wisdom. For a nose there is curly symbol that looks like a question mark. This is the Nepali character for the number 1, which symbolizes unity of all things as well as the one way to reach enlightenment.

As with all other Hindu and Buddhist shrines, you go clockwise around stupas, the natural flow of the cosmos, circling the holy spot or image, the centre of life; you gain enlightenment and amass good karma of the body, the mind and the soul by circumambulating a stupa. Go anti-clockwise and you generate bad karma.

It is also believed all the devas and dragons, yakshas (nature spirits) and ghosts, will approach and make good offerings and not harm you if you circle around the stupa clockwise.

I know all this now, but when I first set foot in the square I pointed - with my red devil left hand - to a temple that fascinated me and headed anti-clockwise around the stupa to get there, until my rickshaw driver gently tugged me in the opposite direction by my right hand and explained.

This square is a main pilgrimage site in the old part of Thamel. We come across a pagoda temple devoted to Harti, the goddess of smallpox. Prayer wheels, mini stupas and statues of deities, and a large golden Buddha looks down at you serenely from a holy shrine at the far end of the square.

There are pigeons here too, masses of them, but they add to the atmosphere and feel to this spot as they do in London. A little lad grabs my attention and heart; bucket in hand amongst the pigeons feeding them. I've often thought of him since, been haunted by him, and prayed that he is safe and sound.

I walk back to the rickshaw with the man, we cycle on and soon arrive at Durbar Square. The second my feet hit the ground the rickshaw owner introduces me to a guide to the square, who prompts me over to the booth to pay my entrance fee. I assume the price of this includes this guide too, it doesn't I discover later, but his knowledge of the history of place and each building is fantastic and invaluable, so I'm happy to part with dollars at the end.

First I'm greeted by the fearsome looking six-armed multi-coloured Kala Bhairab - a manifestation of the god Shiva - that wears a headband of skulls, is using severed heads as weapons and a corpse lies at its feet. Local criminals were brought in front of Bhairab to confess, if they told a lie they believed Bhairab would kill them.

I'm guided around in a dream, looking up in awe at the ancient temples, the old palaces of the kings of Kathmandu, several originate back to the 12th century. My guide shows me an old wooden building.

'This is the Kathmandu House, Kathmandu mean wooden house, this is the original.'

Inside are rare images of the god Gorakhnath. A plaque inside says the building dates back to 1048 making it one of the oldest in Nepal. A holy man sits in one corner, with his wife, I'd guess, at his side; my guide takes me over to him. 'He'll give you a blessing.'

I kneel before him; the holy man says a few words and imprints a red tilaka mark in the middle of my forehead.

'Give him some rupees,' instructs my guide.

Next I'm drawn to an old bent and twisted tree in the heart of the square. I love trees and this is one of the very best I've ever seen, it wouldn't look out of place in a Grimm fairytale or growing out of the imagination of JRR Tolkien. This is a holy Bodhi tree, said to be a descendant from the very tree that Buddha sat under and found enlightenment. A small brick enclosure sits within the base of its wide trunk, inside are bronze casts of Buddha's feet.

Every which way you turn there is an architectural delight of faiths and ancient history. The tallest temple in the square is the Trailokya Mohan Narayan dedicated to Vishnu. A 17th century octagonal Krishna temple sits in another corner. On a platform are two huge old drums that were used to beat out a warning, the armoury is nearby. There's a three-tiered Vishnu temple.

Many of the intricate temple carvings on the roof struts in Durbar Square depict scenes of erotic art and the next building my guide takes me to is full of them, not just on the roof struts but all over the building graphic depictions of tantric sex are portrayed. 'The Kama Sutra temple,' he smiles.

He then points to a small strange figure, red robed and hooded, looking like some crazy little alien Jedi from *Star Wars*. 'That's the Hanuman, the monkey god, his face is covered because he doesn't want to see the sin that goes on at the Karma Sutra temple,' he informs me.

'Hear no, speak no, see no evil,' I reply, but it seems lost on him.

We walk on through an entrance to a large courtyard, surrounded by grand old buildings, pagoda shaped towers soar above, Nasal Chowk, once the palace grounds of the old Kings until 1896. Coronations took place on this spot, as recently as 2001, when King Gyanendra was crowned, the last King of Nepal. His accession to the throne came under the dark shadow of the Nepalese royal massacre. In the June of that year, his brother, Birendra, who was the King of Nepal at the time, was killed along with Queen Aishwarya and seven others by the heir to the throne, Prince Dipendra.

The monarchy are no longer rulers of Nepal. By the time of Gyanendra's coronation the Nepalese Civil War had already been raging since 1996; initiated by the Maoist Communist Party of Nepal. In 2006 they joined forces with their former opposition of government politicians and ousted the monarchy.

Back out in Durbar Square I'm taken to the Maju Deval temple: a pyramid of steps lead up to an imposing tower. For any music loving Englishman this is a favourite spot.

'This became known as the hippie temple, The Beatles, Jimi Hendrix, Pink Floyd and others came here, sat on those steps,' my guide informs me.

'Wow.'

'This was the main place for western hippies to gather and smoke marijuana in the late 60's, many lived or stayed on that street over there,' he points to a street leading off the square. 'It was called Freak Street.'

My mind goes back to when I was a little kid, my dad was always talking about a kaftan coat wearing hippie he worked with called Jeff, 'Hippie Jeff,' (who had a fantastic record collection), I recall Kathmandu being mentioned several times. I wonder if he is still around? I would love to talk to him about those days.

I know Freak Street was a Mecca on the Hippie Trail of the late 60's and 70's, full of hashish shops. Many settled there, until the government of Nepal cracked down on drugs and the lifestyle and dress code of the Hippies, deporting them to India (many returned, though).

My guide saves the best until last: through an elaborately carved wooden entrance we enter into a small courtyard. More intricately carved wooden buildings surround us on all sides, little glassless windows in each, some with shutters. In the ones at the back you catch a glimpse of dolls. For it's within these walls the little living goddess, the Kumari, resides. I've read about this spot, if you're very lucky she may put in an appearance at the small square open window in the middle of the building facing the entrance to the courtyard. But if she does, under no circumstances must you take her picture, this is strictly forbidden, big signs in all major languages of the world clearly states this. I take a few shots of the courtyard and then respectfully slip my camera away into my pocket, cross my fingers and gaze up at the window wishing for her to appear.

The Kumari are young pre-adolescent girls that are worshipped as manifestations of the divine female Durga (warrior goddess). They remain in the role until she menstruates, after which it is believed that the goddess vacates her body. The selection process is vigorous: picked at first for their natural beauty aged around 4 or 5 – from the Newari Shakya caste (the clan to which the Buddha belonged).

Amongst the attributes the potential Kumari must possess are: a neck like a conch shell, a body like a banyan tree, eyelashes like a cow, thighs like a deer, chest like a lion, voice soft and clear as a duck's. Her hair and eyes should be black, and she should have dainty hands and feet.

They are then tested for their inner strength and spirituality. Taken into a courtyard of the Taleju Temple, the little girl has the ghastly encounter of seeing the severed heads of sacrificed animals, illuminated by candlelight, as scary looking masked men dance around, and she must not flinch, weep or cry out or show any fear. She's then left in a darkened room with more goat and buffalo heads.*

If the little girl has shown serenity and fearlessness she becomes the living goddess the Kumari, dressed mainly in elaborate dresses of red and gold. She moves into the Kumari Bahal, only leaving this for ceremonial occasions a few times each year and then her feet must not touch the ground, she's carried in a golden chariot amongst her people, who worship her.

*When I told Irish Tom about the Kumari and severed heads, he replied, with the dry delivery that Irish comedian Dara O Briain would have been proud of. 'Maybe she's just a psychopath.' I have to admit I was in tension relieving (it was after the earthquake) hysterics when he came out with this.

Legend tells that the Kumari tradition started under the rule of King Jayaprakash Malla, the last Nepalese King of the Malla Dynasty (12th–17th century CE). A red serpent came to his chambers with the goddess Taleju, she offered him and his country protection. They played games together in secret, he was not to tell anyone of their meetings, but one day the King's wife discovered them. Taleju fled, telling the King that if he wanted to see her again she would be found among the Newari (Shakya) community, incarnated as a little girl. The current host of Taleju's spirit is the Royal Kumari of Kathmandu, Matina Shakya.

There's only my guide and me, and a few other tourists, in the courtyard to begin with, not enough to entice her out. Soon, though, a party of 10 or so Chinese tourists filter in. My guide and a couple of other Nepalese present gently call up to her, a minute or so pass and then….

There she is! Dressed all in orange, deity make-up surrounded eyes, gazing down, both serene and regal. Alas not for long, one ignorant, selfish, disrespectful, Chinese tourist near the front whips out a camera with a telescopic lens so big it could pick out a flea on Everest and points it up at the Kumari. She's gone in an instant. He turns round with a stupid smile on his face. Shutters open up in the courtyard windows, female courtiers of the little goddess rain down what I hope is verbal abuse on the fool, my guide and other Nepalese shout at him.

'He's upset her now, she won't come out again,' says my guide.

Ah well, it may have only been for 30 seconds or so, but it's forever a divine treasured visitation for me.

I think I've one last architectural treasure to see when my guide takes me down a street at the back of Durbar Square, and up a flight of stairs. But this just leads into his shop, where he makes extra dollars by selling Mandala posters to tourists. I know what's coming and why he's brought me here. He unrolls several and they are beautiful pieces of art and I'm tempted, but as I explain to him, when they're rolled up in the tube I just haven't the space to fit them in my already over crammed rucksack that I'm off to Everest with.

'It'll squeeze in easily,' he insists. 'Protect you from avalanches.'

I have to politely decline best I can. 'When I return, I'll come and buy one,' I reply.

He's seems a little disappointed, but on the walk back into the square he has another dollar making offering. 'Let's hire a taxi, come visit my family, we live high up in the north of Kathmandu, a beautiful view over the city, have dinner, fifty dollar.'

Again I have to decline as firmly but politely as possible. Tell him I have to be at a meeting with my holiday firm, Intrepid, early afternoon. One day with this guy and half my holiday budget will be gone, and when I pay him for his guided tour he seems to suggest that this is not enough either, his face drops.

'Look I'm sorry. I thought the entrance fee included a guided tour. When I get back, I'll come and see you again, I promise, buy a Mandala, maybe visit your family'…

…he'd have been there…that day, and his family lived in the badly hit north of Kathmandu……

My rickshaw rider is waiting for me. 'How much is it so far and to take me back to the Kathmandu Guest House?' I ask.

'Twenty dollar.'

What? He said a few hundred rupees to start with, oh ok maybe this is the going rate. He cycles on. 'We go monkey temple, very special?'

I'm in two minds, I would like to fit in Durbar Square and the Swayambhunath 'monkey temple' today and be free to maybe go to Patan and other old villages and special places of interest on my return from Everest. 'How much?'

'Thirty dollar.'

Hmm, oh sod it, I'll afford myself this luxury, it will be fun being taken through the streets on a rickshaw up to the monkey temple, but I get assurances from him that he'll wait for me.

'Yes he replies as we cycle on, thirty five dollar.' This he repeats over his shoulder several times, like he's a verbal meter, and I'm half expecting it to change up a few dollars around every bend.

We pass some fabulous old curiosity shops on the way. Up in my seat I look down into little wooden open fronted shops and see cobblers and what looks like a watchmaker or silversmith at work, like it's not changed since the time Dickens was wandering into the equivalent in Victorian London.

So we start to climb steadily upwards through narrow streets, then the ascent becomes quite steep. My rickshaw rider has to climb off the cycle and push. I'm from a working-class old coal mining village, it doesn't matter what he's charging me, I can't sit there like some fat, upper class Englishman in the Raj and expect him to sweat his bollocks off trying to push me up a steep hill in his rickshaw. So I jump down and help him push it the rest of the way up to the monkey temple.

'I'll wait, forty dollar,' he announces.

Well, there's gratitude.

He drops me off at the base of the hill on which the stupendous stupa topped Swayambhunath Temple sits. One of the oldest religious sites in Nepal, the stupa is supposed to be one of the oldest in the world; revered by both Buddhists and Hindus. Ancient legend tells that the valley was once filled with water, out of which a giant lotus flower grew that became the hill now known as Swayambhu or 'self-created.' Another legend says the temple was built over an eternal flame.

Swayambhunath adopted the name 'monkey temple' as the sacred primates live here. The origins of this tell of the Manjushree, the Bodhisattva of wisdom and learning, who was creating the hill on which the temple stands, when he decided to grow his hair long. From his hair came lice which transformed into monkeys that have lived on the hill ever since.

I soon encounter rhesus monkeys when stepping forth, slowly, this is the first big test of my fitness, even before reaching the Himalayas, up the steep 365 steps. Before the monkeys however, on the lower sections, you pass by a variety of people trying to sell you their wares. There's also several beggar children, one little girl approaches me waving her deformed hand, it's heartbreaking.

A line of golden Buddhas sit atop a platform. Up you go, a variety of trees grow either side of the steps (Swayambhunath in Tibet translates as 'sublime trees'). From these are draped strings of green, yellow, red, white and blue prayer flags. At either side of the stairway to Buddha heaven are colourfully painted icons. A Nepalese woman with a tray of fruit comes walking down the steps to feed the monkeys, they hop down out of the trees and over the wall to greet her. I pause, resting my hand on top of a stone elephant to get my breath, and look up to see the eyes of Buddha on the stupa - a golden hat atop his head - watching my progress, or is that just my imagination? I follow his real gaze and turn and see the stunning vista of Kathmandu now visible below, stretching off into the hills in the distance.

Up another flight of steps and I'm up amongst the mighty stupa, temples and shrines. I follow a local woman lighting candles and copy her in running my hand down a line of prayer wheels. In a wall recess stands an ancient 7th century Buddha carved from a single piece of black stone, there is none other like it in Nepal. A golden Vajra thunderbolt sits on a round platform covered in animal sculptures; a well is said to be underneath this that reflected the images of the dead. Vajruis is a Sanskrit word meaning both thunderbolt and diamond. Additionally, it is a symbolic ritual object that symbolizes both the properties of a diamond (indestructibility) and a thunderbolt (irresistible force).

I sit for a while on a seat, taking in a view over Kathmandu; in the distance is the huge 203 ft high white tower, Dharahara, a lighthouse for enlightened souls. The sun shines at last, a monkey sits happily chomping on a piece of fruit under a large bell, prayer flags flap in a gentle breeze. A special moment in my time at a special place, sat on my throne in some fantasy Shangri-la kingdom of legend, spiritualised, happy, at peace, my dream holiday starting to be established as just that. It is 11.56 am on April 22nd 2015.

My focus zooms on down into the suburbs, a curious thing, many houses appeared to have an unfinished third or fourth floor to them. At the time I assumed that they build higher when the money becomes available, but Aussie Paul in our group (who you shall meet later) informs me that it's a ploy to beat the building tax laws. You have to pay more for a completed building, but if it is still under construction you pay less, so lots of people just leave their homes in an unfinished state.

I have a wander in and out and around the temples and shrines several times. Then wander off down another set of steps – on a gentler descending slope. Trees arch above, monkeys scurry along the top of walls and buildings. Down this way are masses of prayer flags, a multicolour extravaganza, with another smaller stupa at the bottom and the lime green 'world peace pond,' in the middle of this rises a golden Buddha, spraying water.

I leave the temple of dreams via another flight of steps, here are more beggar children […every day, I bet they're there everyday I'm thinking on April 27th…], out onto a dusty road, pass by 3 enormous golden Buddhas and down to where my rickshaw driver is waiting patiently. He would be, especially when he announces I've run over the time he said he'd wait for me. 'Fifty dollar.'

I've half a mind to do the equivalent of taxi runner (when coming home from a local town, drunk, in my younger years) but finally put my tame foot down. 'Ok OK, but no more, fifty dollar, you'll have to stop at a cash point on the way back to the guest house.'

'Ok fifty dollar.'

On the way up he'd been careful to avoid going up a narrow lane where road workers had dug a trench down the middle of the street. This time he either decides to take the quickest route back down as possible or forgets and takes a wrong turning. He tries to get by the ditch, which has large lumps of rubble at the side that the rickshaw has to bounce over, whilst having to avoid pipping motorcycles. Several times I'm nearly upended and think I'm either going to go flying through the window of one of those old curiosity shops mentioned earlier and spoil a day's work of a craftsman. Or go headfirst into the ditch or under the wheels over a motorbike or taxi. So I jump down and help him push it again. At last we are back in the maze of Thamel, and I'm back in the seat as he speeds up, eager to get his money and be back out in his tourist fishing ground no doubt, ready to lure in another innocent aboard. But you know what, do you think I begrudge paying that fifty dollar now? Never, not with hell's hindsight.

Back at Kathmandu Guest House, the sun still shines, so at last I can go out and fully enjoy the chill-out delights of the oasis garden. There's only a scattering of people in there. I sit at a table and order a cool drink. Then wander over to a far corner of the lawn that is in full sunlight, to lie down and soak it in. There is something that resembles a four poster bed in another corner that looks inviting, but I'm too self conscious to go stretch out on that. Moments later a young, bearded, pony-tailed, ultra trendy young American traveller appears on the seen and has no inhibitions at all, kicking off his shoes, jumping up onto the 'bed,' opening up a book and looking as cool as fuck.

Ah well, I'm happy with my own little corner thanks, until the strong sun begins to burn and I realise I've not smeared on my SPF 30 cream. I go over to sit on a covered rocking bench and gently sway to and fro, imaging John Lennon and Paul McCartney sat in a lotus position on the grass in front of me, conjuring up pop magic in the sun of Kathmandu in the late 60's. I wonder if any of their great songs were first conceived on this very spot? 'Tomorrow Never Knows?' 'Across the Universe?' I listen to these on my iPod. Soon the gentle rocking and my drifting imagination send me drifting off to sleep.

When I open my eyes a blonde woman is sat down at the table at the side of me. We start chatting amiably, her name is Lauren, she's from Australia; nice smile, easy to talk to, great sense of humour and it quickly transpires she's part of my group on the Intrepid Everest Base Camp trip too. A big, thick set white guy comes and sits nears us, and I guess he could be part of our group too, the way he looks across when he picks up on part of our conversation.

The clock ticks around to 2.30 pm, the time set for our Intrepid meet up and talk. Lauren and me have a wander inside, the white guy follows us and introduces himself, Paul, who sounds cockney to my northern ears, but is from Kent. He appears to be another sound person. Great that's now 3 people I'm sure I'll get on with, 12 to meet. Most of the others are already sat around tables in a back room, being addressed by a Nepalese guy; this is Lalit our trek leader. Formalities over we're all asked to introduce ourselves.

We have the ones already mentioned, Irish Tom, Aussie Lauren, Southern Paul and myself. Also present and seemingly correct are Chandler and Annabelle: two 19-year-old, handsome and beautiful gap year students. Chandler is from Canada, a sports enthusiast, working for a golfing firm. Annabelle was born in Australia, but brought up and currently living in Hong Kong. Soon she's off to University in the U.S.A. A grey haired chap with glasses, sat with his wife, tells us his name is Paul, an Australian sheep farmer. His wife isn't going with us, she's off to stay with Paul's sister, Janne, who's a nun up at Kopan Monastery (situated high on a hill on the edges of Kathmandu, one of the must-see places to visit I'd read on TripAdvisor).

Nick is a quietly spoken, young Canadian man, with hair tied back in a ponytail and dark olive skin, his family having originated from Guyana. Dave is a cheeky faced Scot about in his late 20's or early 30's. Suntana 'sunny' Moh and Gae are two lovely women from Bangkok. Mel, short blonde hair, glasses, in her 30's, is a doctor from Australia. At first she comes across as a know-all, the way she keeps butting in to Lalit's trek talk, but we soon learn there is substance to what she says (and not someone who's read up on every single aspect of the trip and wants to show off the point) as she now lives and does great work as a doctor in an area near Kathmandu. Her stream of facts can seem relentless at times and sometimes not entirely tactful, but she'll turn out to be one of the most invaluable members of the group in the end, her heart in the right place you realise and everyone will warm to her.

Stephanie is surprisingly the only American in the group. She's quite laidback and has a sharp sardonic humour, sharpened after a time living in London. Rahul is a quiet Indian gentlemen, a family man and owns a textile business.

Last but by no means least is Dave, originally form Canada, the definite standout character. About 40 or 50 something (I can't quite figure his age), a stars and stripes bandanna atop his shaven head, back-to-front baseball cap on top of this, two gold teeth, tattoos, a Bad Religion t-shirt showing a woman in bondage gear. An ex marine, with Native American blood, animated both physically and verbally, I nickname him, in my head, Hard Easy Rider. Yet he lives in Burnley, Lancashire, England, which is a match I could never find in heaven in a million years. The 16th member of the group was to be Hard Easy Rider's 'fitness instructor' apparently, but he pulled out. All in all it seems like a fine group to me, 13 solo trekkers, plus the two Thai women, of various ages from a variety of countries, just what I was hoping for.

After setting out the trek details for us Lalit suggests we all meet up later, in the evening, for the real easy going, getting to know you party at a western style restaurant, just down from the guest house. Here Aussie Paul sits to my left, Thai Gae across from me and Scot's Dave to my right. The latter is the next one I started getting into conversation with, well try to, at first his broad, fast Glaswegian accent is gobbledegook to me. But he seems very friendly and funny and so I smile and nod to begin with. Soon, like a British accent Babel fish has been dropped into my ear, I start tuning into his voice patterns. Yes he is funny, smart, friendly and well travelled, which I love hearing about. Before coming to Kathmandu he did a flying visit to India, but panicked as his passport and visa didn't come back from their embassy until a few days before setting off. He informs me that the traffic, hustle and bustle out on the streets of Kathmandu (that I deem to be crazy) is sedate compared to India.

Annabelle tells me she's been in Kathmandu before, working at an orphanage. I feel humbled, still only 19 she has such an assured, nice, open-minded and caring nature.

Aussie Paul seems a true gent, down to earth and easy going. And when I strike up conversation with Thai Gae she's sweet and shy behind a wide welcoming smile.

We're all soon back to the Kathmandu Guest House and bed as we have an early start and long day ahead the following day; a 6.30 am flight into the Himalayas, landing at Lukla, then we start trekking. I have very little sleep, excitement and adrenalin starting to pump, the pigeons falling out over the best roosting spot outside the window and now I share a room; with Aussie Paul, and at times he snores like a 747 coming into land.

We chatted for while before getting our heads down, and I've no doubt he's a thoroughly nice guy; calm, measured and thoughtful. He talks with obvious pride of his land and sheep farm back in Australia; only 100 acres, small by that countrie's standards, but you can tell it makes him a very contented man, along with the love for his wife, children and country. With my ignorant English view of Australia, i.e. a mostly orange wasteland, apart from a small number of famous cities, and the *Home and Away* style coastal areas, I'm surprised when he tells me that where his farm is located (not far from Melbourne, near

Orange City) it has four distinct seasons, including snow in winter. As he paints a picture of being up in the hills there, I can almost feel the sense of solitude and peace he revels in. I mention my solitary walks; with my sheep dog (although Flossy has no interest in sheep at all) up into the quiet of the green English hills where I live, and the relaxing peace I find there.

Being a true blooded Australian man Paul loves his sport: cricket, rugby. He watches the kind of airplane races that could only take place in big countries like Australia and America: customised World War 2 planes, Spitfires, Mustangs etc, racing around a circuit in the air, only 50ft off the ground in places. Paul mentions his love for motorbike racing too, so we talk of the Moto GP and Australia World Champion Casey Stoner. And now I can boast about my village's motorbike credentials: Barry Sheen's team-mate John Newbold came from Jacksdale, so did TT racer Steve Henshaw, and now we have a motorbike whizkid, Kyle Ryde, who is starting to take the sport by storm. His career began like Casey Stoner by winning the 100cc Championship, but Ryde did so younger than the Aussie hero and broke all records before him, he then won the Superstock championship at his first attempt and now in his first season in Supersport is leaving seasoned riders in his wake. Still only 17, a future World Champion in the waiting, I write down his name for Paul.

As mentioned earlier Paul's wife was visiting his sister, Janne, a nun at Kopan Monastery, before going off exploring the attractions around Kathmandu, whilst Paul is on the Everest Base Camp trek. Paul has already been up to the monastery and tells me all about the place. It sounds magical and strengthens my desire to go there on our return to Kathmandu. Added to his description of the buildings, monks and gardens is the fact that a key Lama connected to the monastery is due to visit in a few days time and will be staying for a few weeks. Paul's sister has been helping prepare his room; he shows me pictures of it, lavishly decorated with Buddhist iconography, situated on top of the senior monk's quarters with its own roof top garden.

The night is ticking on, time for bed. I have the last shower I'm expecting for a while and the last shave I intend to have until my quest is done, well I've got to look the part walking back into my local pub in England. 'Oh the beard, well I've just come back from an expedition to Everest.'

The following are my photos of Kathmandu, Thamel, Durbar Square and Swayambhunath 'monkey temple,' taken on a beautiful sunny day April 22nd 2015.

Thamel, Kathmandu, the evening of April 21st 2015.

Above: Garuda statue.
Top right: Maju Deval 'the hippie temple.' Bottom right: Basantapur, Royal Palace.

Above: Holy couple inside the 11th century 'Kathmandu House,' Durbar Square.

Buddhist stupa at Swayambhunath, 'the monkey temple.'

Thurs Apr 23rd 2015, Kathmandu, Lukla, the Himalayas:

I'm already awake by the time my alarm goes off at 5.00 am, ready for the early flight to Lukla. We're not flying there from Kathmandu International; we board a smaller aircraft of 'Yeti Airlines' from a smaller domestic airport. When we arrive the place is a building site; we line up for our flight down a rubble strewn corridor between half constructed rooms, I lean on a wall and get white paint on my new black, 3 in 1, hiking jacket. We try not to pass under the builder's ladders and have to move aside for said builders clocking on for the day's graft. Two fur tangled, dusty, street dogs join us in the queue, they look friendly enough, even quite cute. A couple of smitten women in our group move to make a fuss of them, but Mel interjects with one of her vital facts.

'Don't stroke them, they'll be infested with fleas, and don't feed them, if you do that they'll try and follow you onto the plane.'

At least the departure lounge is still in its old complete state. The security here is a brief body check, a metal detector gate that often beeps but is often ignored and a series of graphic signs on the departure counter that shows pictures of prohibited items, like a dog with cross through it and also a gun. This stating of the bleeding obvious tickles Lauren and me.

'Damn I have to leave my gun toting street dog behind,' she laughs.

'Someone is going to be disappointed when they turn up with their T Rex on a lead and see the picture of a dinosaur with a forbidden cross through it,' I come in with.

'Perhaps they allow Yetis given the name of the airline, don't see a picture denying them a passage home.'

So we're all set to take a flight to the Tenzing-Hillary Airport at Lukla 'the most dangerous airport in the world' (in a Channel 4 series *The World's Most Extreme: Runways* it was listed at no.2, only a military runway in war-torn Afghanistan topped it). Lukla has a narrow runway, running uphill, cut into a hillside at the edge of the Himalayan Mountains. In the last 7 years there have been 4 crashes with 32 people losing their lives, passengers like us, off Everest bound. With all my mum's worries I'd thought it best not to mention this.

Aussie Paul has some reassuring words, though, the plane we are travelling on is a De Havilland Canada DHC-6 Twin Otter, old but incredibly robust and reliable…..the same plane that crashed at Lukla in 2008, killing 18 people that I'd read about. There was diverse weather conditions that day, though, heavy fog and the pilot came in too low. And it turns out I don't feel as nervous on this flight as I did on the landing at Kathmandu in a big modern passenger plane; that suffered punchy turbulence going through storm clouds. It could be the incredible distraction we have from thoughts of a potentially perilous landing. This may be considered a dangerous flight, but it also must be one of the most beautiful in the world; I'd read this and remembered to position myself on the left side of the plane. Out the window, the lush valleys of Nepal drift by, but the breathtaking factor is the view of the glistening snow capped Himalayan Mountain chain out to the left. Stunning, it is a little hazy but many peaks are visible, I wonder if one is Everest?*

*Yes it was, just visible. I'd only realise this months later on taking another look at my photo from the plane window.

40

There is one moment of shivers down the spine, when the aircraft seems to be heading for a mountain side, but then it veers to the right and descends on down to Lukla, a hop, skip and a bounce and we're safely on Himalayan terra firma.

A group of local Nepalese people gather outside the flimsy tiny airport security fence, watching on, like they never get tired of the spectacle of airplanes landing on the narrow runway, even though they live here.

Luggage retrieved, we make our way by the locals, there are a few warm 'Namaste's' exchanged, as we walk up a path and into Lukla village. With snowy mountains behind and the style of architecture it almost resembles somewhere in the Alps, if built on a very tight budget, a lot poorer. Some of the shop owners selling vital gear, souvenirs, food and drinks must do well here, though, with the thousands of trekkers and mountaineers starting out on their Everest adventures during the two main seasons of the year. There are a scattering of hotels, internet cafes, and even Irish and Scottish bars. At the far end of the village you do encounter the simple dwellings of the locals, and of course dogs are everywhere again.

We stop here at a restaurant for breakfast. Lalit gives us more trek information and it's time to meet our porters. They line up before us, young healthy looking Nepalese mountain men, each tells us his name in turn and where they are from and how many days they have had to walk to get here, 1, 2, 3, 4, 5! This is met by 'wows' and applause from our group at the end of the introduction. Several are genuine Sherpas, and I learn for the first time that this means they are an ethnic group that migrated from Tibet some 300 or 400 years back, Sherpa means 'eastern people.' Of course they are most revered for their mountaineering skills; no expedition to summit Everest would be ready without Sherpas in their group with their expert knowledge of the region, climbing skill, strength and endurance. As the books of man's great achievements tell, the most famous of Sherpas is Tenzing Norgay who with Sir Edmund Hillary became the first people to summit Everest in 1953.

After our meal and introduction I go to the bar to get a coke. I'm wearing my Manchester United top, which is fully on show now the weather is warm and my jacket is off. The Nepalese lad behind the counter greets me with a big smile. 'English?' He asks.

'Yeah.'

'I love the Premiership,' he looks down at my shirt with disdain. 'Not that shirt though.'

'Why not?'

'I'm a Liverpool fan.'

We both laugh. 'I can't get away from my rivals, even up in the Himalayas,' I say.

We shake hands and part in good humour. Now with our porters in place to carry our heavy luggage and guide us (and be great company as it turns out), food in our bellies, the water in our 1ltr bottles purified, we gather together and at last set forth for Everest Base Camp.

At the edge of Lukla is a kani and an arch memorial to Pasang Lhamu, the first Nepali woman to climb Everest in 1993. In front of this we pause for a group photograph, the EBC class of April 2015. The trail begins on passing through the arch, we walk on, hopefully not through any more unseasonable storms, and you have to hold your head up high in this towering part of the world. The Liverpool loving Sherpa would be happy, I've their anthem in my head.

Following the route of the exquisite, turquoise and frothy white coloured Dudh Koshi river 'the milky river,' along an ancient trading route from Tibet, down and up the side of high wooded valley sides, mountains peering down, I'm already in paradise; this section alone would suffice as a class walking holiday.

In sections we pass clockwise round mani stones, inscribed with Buddhist mantras. The trail is fairly busy, mainly with local traffic, mule and yak trains. There's the tinkling of the bells, hung around the animal's necks, and the shout will go up of 'safe side,' our guides gesturing for us to press back safely out of the way and let them pass. The yaks have fearsome looking horns but seem sedate enough. Aussie Paul tells me that these are a cross between cows and yaks and that the real hairy yaks up in the high mountains may not be so friendly. And I'm not too sure about the tolerance of these half-breeds either, as a little later I make the mistake of overtaking a yak, on the danger side, and get nudged by its horns too near the edge and a drop way down into a ravine.

I'm soon encountering those colourful rhododendrons that lured me to do the trek at this time of year; bushes of brilliant red, pink or purple flowers in full bloom. Up high on the valley sides whole clusters of them grow giving brilliant splashes of colour, oh Turner, Monet and Van Gogh, you didn't get to paint all the wonders of the natural world.

The walking is not too strenuous at this stage, but climbing up one long steep section I'm sure glad I put the months in getting fit, with heart pumping runs up to Codnor Castle and the long walks down the Erewash Valley (that resembles a 1 tenth model valley in a model village compared to these lush high sided swathes leading to the highest mountains on earth).

Irish Tom appears to be trekking along no more out of breath than me, though, and he appears slightly overweight and had told me that his decision to go on a holiday trekking to Everest Base Camp had been a spontaneous decision, made just about a month ago and that he'd done no training at all.

And up front of our line, like they're having an easy Sunday afternoon stroll in the park, even on the steepest sections, day after day, young Annabelle and Chandler chat away, shedding no sweat or having to gasp for any breath. They seem made for each other on this trip; like they've been friends or childhood sweethearts for years. We all think it's sweet, but Annabelle has a boyfriend, a handsome Swedish guy she later shows a photo of to me, and refers to Chandler as like a brother by the end of our time together. Maybe that's true, but I'm not the only one to wonder how their futures will pan out and if it will be together? As unforeseen circumstances unfold they'll definitely form a bond that will never be fully broken I'm sure. Then again we will all become bound together for eternity, by a shared experience none of us could have predicted.

One of the enjoyable aspects of the long day's walking is moving up and down the line chatting to various members of our group and Sherpa guides. One of the latter, Phurba, moves along my side for a while. He loves my Manchester United shirt, wants to know if I go to watch them and listens enthralled when I tell him about my days as a Stretford Ender (the famous terrace stand behind the net at Old

Trafford). Then I'm the one enthralled, in awe, as he tells me about his love of football: Wayne Rooney is his hero, he models his style of play on him, Phurba is a striker he tells me, top scorer in his team. He shows me a picture of them, they wear the home, red, Manchester United shirt. The power of football to reach and inspire all corners of the world. The team photo shows them proudly showing off a cup they've won. This against a number of teams that had travelled from far and wide to compete in the competition; Phurba tells me his team can walk for three days to play a match! I look at him in wonder, the more I hear about these people, the more I'm in their company, my respect grows for them in mountain leaps, day after day.

Phurba is excited about the major competition coming up in May, the Everest Gold Cup, down at the small football ground in Lukla. Many teams from many miles around will compete for this prestigious trophy, Phurba is confident of his team's chances. The opening match is on May 29th; the anniversary of Sherpa Tenzing and Sir Edmund Hillary's summit of Everest. I wish Phurba and his United team success.

We arrive at our teahouse for the night. With many hours of daylight left, Lalit suggests doing one of two acclimatization walks on offer: a circuit high up around near the valley top, or a climb up to a small monastery. Most of us agree on the latter. This is a long, steep climb up many stone steps that tests the legs, my back, heart and lungs, but we do stop for breathers along the way.

Near the base of the walk we encounter a wild eyed woman living in a cave, fire lit, food on, all her worldly belongings gathered around her. 'She's half crazy,' one of our Sherpas says to us. It's sad to think she may have become an outcast from her village because of mental illness and deemed of no use, or has she chosen this abode of her own volition? McCartney's fool in (rather than on) the hill, seeing the world clearer than anyone else gives her credit for, safe in her cave when her mad predictions of the earth shaking and buildings collapsing comes true.

We stop half way up the trail to the monastery and have a wonderful view of the turquoise Dudh Koshi, snaking its way down through the valley. Then I look up, a window has opened in the clouds high above the valley, it stays open long enough just to glimpse it, my first big WOW moment. Way on up there is a mountain! *Way* on up there, the first of the giants, Mt Thamserku, 6,608 m tall (21,680 ft). Speechless I gaze up at it in awe, and point it out to the rest of the group; then the mountain, uninterested in the ants below, puts its head back in the clouds. Excitement ripples through me in anticipation of meeting the Thamserku's big brothers and their mighty mother.

Fairly exhausted we take the last steps up to a tumbledown little monastery in a clearing in the woods on a rocky plateau. It's quite a modest little place, but that makes it feel more authentic, not having the overseas money invested in it like the big lavish and famous monasteries in Kathmandu. A few birds swoop by, all is silent, no one appears to be around. Until, one after another, three tiny child monks appear, dusty robes, shy smiles, the littlest one, bare footed, is carrying two golden candle holders that are nearly as big as he is; he disappears behind a bright yellow and blue decorative flag covering a door. One of the other little monks urges us to follow him through the curtain too, after removing our boots. Inside is a magic little prayer hall, full of colour, golden Buddhas and iconography. We're all enchanted by these little monks in their secluded place of peace and worship. At the end of the day Lalit will ask us of our favourite moment so far; I'll say the mighty mountain putting in an appearance and the mini monastery on the hill.

I go to bed in a state of nirvana, but sleep little, as adrenalin and excitement are now flowing through me with the vibrancy and power of the sweet Dudh Koshi River. When I do enter a make-believe slumber land, I dream I'm on a magic carpet, pulled along through the clouds by a harnessed golden eagle, a mini monk is at the reigns, he turns and points excitedly, 'Everest.' But before I see the object of his excitement, a thunderous snore from Paul awakens me. Ah well, the reality of these Himalayan days are living daydreams. And all being well I'll soon see Everest with my own wide awake eyes.

Fri April 24th 2015, the trek to Namche Bazaar:
After breakfast we set off on a 9km 6 hour walk to the mountain the town of Namche Bazaar. It's quite clear to begin with but clouds over too quickly for my liking, this is still not the usual weather patterns I'd read about for this time of the year, i.e. clear and sunny in the morning, giving a great view of the mountains, then possible clouding over in the late afternoon. The cloud doesn't detract from the beauty of the surroundings, but by the end of the day we're going to at last be in a place of spectacular mountain views, weather permitting. Luckily the sun does come out for a while around dinnertime.

We have to cross several wire suspension bridges this day, each one higher than the last. Hard Easy Rider Dave is freaking out. 'Whoa, way too high man, I'm not a fuckin' bird, I'd vomit a waterfall, if I'd eaten anything, not trying that, I've been shittin' through the eye of a needle.' He stands at the entrance to the bridge, the knees of his tattooed (he's wearing shorts) covered legs trembling. 'Come on guy meditate – MED-I-FUCKIN-TATE,' he says to himself.

I suffer from vertigo too, always have, I even nearly passed out and toppled over the edge to my doom when trying to walk along 'the giddy edge' at the top of the Heights of Abraham at Matlock Bath in Derbyshire (about 10 miles from where I live). But I faced up to my fear more when I went hiking up in the Highlands of Scotland in May 2014; although I did have to shuffle along on my arse on the narrow curving trails up in the high Quiraing ridge (just drop in a fact here, the rocks there are older than the Himalayas, some of the oldest rocks on earth, but they stopped growing, whilst the likes of Everest are still growing up).

It always seems that if I'm high up but in a safe enclosed environment - i.e. I went up over 800ft to the viewing platform of The Shard in London last autumn and felt fine as was behind glass. If, however I'm up high, and it doesn't even have to be that high at all, and it's open to the elements and the drop back to earth, then I'm a nervous wreck, go dizzy. There's the thought of just how easy it would be to fall over the edge or small barrier or wall to your doom, life snuffed out as easy as that, and this unfathomable urge to do just that. Like some depressed suicidal devil is sat on my shoulder: 'Go on, one jump and you break on through to the other side, you get to fly for a few seconds man, jump.'

Yet, inexplicably, I've not felt vertigo on the suspension bridges at all, even though they're open to the elements, are getting very high up above the valley, have slats that you can look down hundreds of feet to the river below and hand rails that my doom devil could easily hop over. I guess it's because I'm so focused and determined to do this trek, and have been right back to January, that I'm finding some inner fear factor quelling resolve not to be a wussy. Maybe it's the calming Buddha effect?

Until Hard Easy Rider Dave shatters my force field by deciding the best way to combat his fear of heights is to get across the 'damn suspense bridges' as quick as possible by running.

'Out of the way guys, Himalayan shit powered rocket coming through,' he shouts sweeping passed me – half way along the bridge – like a tattooed, bandana and baseball cap wearing road runner, causing the bridge to sway alarmingly from side to side.

I looked down to steady my feet, down through the slats to Dudh Koshi way below, looking like a turquoise snake wrapping around its prey in the blur of see saw movements. My stomach churns over, 'down down you drag me down,' sings the devil on my shoulder. I grip the iron side rails, knuckles white, and focus on the prayer flags guiding me to the other end of the bridge, where Hard Easy Rider Dave has summoned up his Native American ancestors and is doing a war dance of triumph.

Mel drops one of her facts in, assuring us that the wires holding up the bridges are set deep in concrete foundations and could carry far more weight than a group of lily-livered western trekkers made up of water, skinny skin and bone. And as to prove her point, at that very moment a heavily laden mule train moves onto the bridge on the far side. Yep cool hard facts, but the human mind in phobia and fear mode doesn't work that way and as Hard Easy Rider Dave and me round another bend in the valley and see another bridge even higher up, we run our hands down every prayer wheel we encounter.

For a while I'm walking with big Southern Paul and getting to know him better. He has a wife and four kids back home. Paul works for a firm that offer sports hospitality packages for some of the biggest events in British and World sport: he informs me that ring side tickets for the Floyd Mayweather vs Manny Pacquiao 'fight of the century' (taking place on May 2nd) have been going for $30,000. The rugby union internationals at Twickenham are his main field, he's been to many a 6 Nations match there and tells me of an after match fund raising do he worked at. Guest of honour was James Bond, Daniel Craig, but he'd chosen to wear not his sharp, secret agent, suit for this event, but a pair of jeans. This didn't go down well with man mountain Martin Johnson, who stormed over, stirred and told a shaken Craig firmly not to wear jeans in that club again. Paul has been inspired to come on this trek as he has friends who are up at Everest Base Camp preparing to make an attempt to summit Everest.

We trek on up through a wooded valley side, then out into an opening with a shimmering waterfall falling from upon high, framed by vibrantly coloured rhododendron bushes, above white fluffy clouds drift over snowy mountain tops. Soon we reach the village of Monjo; a little Nepalese lad sat on a wall gives us all a high five to welcome us. Here the entrance to Sagarmatha National Park is situated, we stop for lunch.

There is a small temple with paintings of Vajrapani, Avalokiteshvara, Manjushri on the wall and a mandala of Avalokiteshvara on the ceiling. Lalit takes us into a little museum that has a 3D model map of the Himalayan Mountains.

We sit out in the warm sun, looking on in disbelief as the Nepalese equivalent of extra wide heavy loads pass by: no roads or lorries or railways here, men (and women too carry loads that would be back breaking to the average western male) are the means of transport for many goods; the lucky ones have boxes of Pringles – that seem to be extremely popular in these parts – piled on their backs, but several pass by carrying an unbelievable amount of beer cases. 'They can carry between 91 to 100kg's on their backs,' Lalit informs us. It's a hard living, a hard existence, their average life expectancy is 45.

Hard Easy Rider Dave is chatting about his reasons and aims of going to Everest Base Camp. His mother has recently passed away. 'The damp cold English winter finished her.' He plans to leave a photograph of her there, along with prayer flags. My heart goes out to him, even more so as he reveals more. He'd been living with his mother (it must have been a council house and I don't fully understand or hear how they ended up living in such circumstances in Burnley, England), after her death the authorities told him he couldn't live there any more. 'Nice, huh, fuck em, I'll be a gypsy, I'm travelling here then I'll do the Camino de Santiago.'

I'd never heard of that trek, an old pilgrim way, of St James, from France over the Pyrenees on to remote areas of north-west Spain, ending at the Cathedral of Santiago de Compostela in Galicia, until I saw the film *The Way* starring Martin Sheen just a few months back: the story of how the bohemian son of Sheen's character (a stiff shirted conservative doctor) dies shortly after setting off on the Camino. The doctor decides to complete the Camino Way in his memory; along the way he finds enlightenment and meets a host of colourful characters. Hard Easy Rider Dave could easily have been one of them, a script writer's dream.

I'd actually thought of the film when I'd booked the Everest Base Camp trek and learned there would be 15 other people in my trekking group. Will I encounter some crazy and memorable characters? I wondered. Well Hard Easy Rider Dave is certainly that and it just happens he's doing the Camino Way next!

He's also not looking too well, still 'shitting through the eye of a needle,' not eating, off his food. And a short while after lunch, I notice he is missing. We've entered the Sagarmatha Park and start the 2000ft trek up to Namche Bazaar, the sun disappears; grey cloud moves in, our waterproofs are on as a fine rain falls. Concerned I ask Lalit where he is.

'He flew off, way ahead,' he tells me.

Half an hour later on, I'm out of breath, taking the last steps up onto a little rocky plateau, where a mani stone, temple, little shops and toilets are located, an ideal place to rest a while. Hard Easy Rider Dave is already there, looking relaxed, lying on the grass, 'backy' roll up hanging out of his mouth.

'How did you get up here so fast?' I ask.

'Meditation man, took myself in the zone, when I came to I was here.'

Irish Tom and Scot's Dave are asking about my writing, when we set off again, particularly my book *If the Kids are United*, talk gets around to the Hillsborough Disaster chapter, I recount my experiences of that April day.

*

The approach to Namche is up a steep path cut into the right side of a very deep, mist filled valley; cliffs and rocky outcrops on the far side. A huge griffon vulture sweeps majestically by at eye level. I'd seen pictures of Namche online and couldn't wait to arrive here: a cluster of buildings, mainly teahouses, larger hotels and shops - this being the last main stop off town before Everest - hanging onto two steep hillsides with a magnificent line of huge snowy mountains above. Alas these are lost in cloud when we arrive – clockwise around a white and golden stupa – this rainy day. But again we receive a warm welcome; up in a huge open window to a stone building, some 15ft up, stood a little girl dancing around, singing and shouting down 'Namaste!' to any trekker entering the town.

'Namaste!' we shouted back, waving, big smiles put on our tired faces.

Most of the group are ready to tuck into a well deserved meal after an arduous long day trekking, but I'm feeling sick, tired and dizzy. Maybe it's just lack of sleep and exhaustion? Or it could be what I've been dreading, the early symptoms of altitude sickness? I only eat a few of my cheese momos and barely touch the apple pie at all, but do knock back plenty of water and a Diamox pill, I'm taking no chances.

I'd been happy-go-lucky and chatty on the trip so far but disappear into a fuzzy shell for a while. Several of the group are concerned, including our trek leader Lalit, he asks how I'm feeling then takes mine and the rest of the group's blood pressure and heart rate, and I'm relieved when he gives me a thumbs up, mine seem perfectly normal.

Soon, after a Mars Bar, more water and the effects of the Diamox kicking in, I'm feeling back to more of my old self again, joining several of the group heading down into the narrow old stone streets of Namche. It's market day: under a tarpaulin cover steam rises as a man and woman make what looks like popcorn in a huge dish, stall holders sell fruit, drinks, western snacks, colourful clothing, cloth and loads of wonderful souvenirs. I eye a few I'd like to buy - a variety of prayer wheels and Buddhas - but aware that I've very little, if any, room in my bags to place fairly delicate objects at this stage, I plan to wait until we pass through this way on the way back from Everest.

We all gather in the canteen area of teahouse for the rest of the night. In there are a middle-aged German couple who have summited Everest in the past. They tell of one terrifying incident when an avalanche crashed over their tent. I mention the BBC news report (on just before I flew out to Nepal) about the devastating avalanche in April 2014 that killed 16 people, mainly Sherpas. Aussie Paul says a family friend is a helicopter pilot in the Himalayas and was involved in the rescue attempt and how he had brought bodies back from Everest.

Just about everyone in our EBC group goes up to bed for an early night, but knowing I'll not sleep before 12.00 am I stay down in the company of the Sherpas. Rahul is still up too and I chat to him a while, about his family, cricket and why football has never taken off in India (the climate just doesn't suit). He's a likable, self effacing guy but so laid back it's like he's not there at times, when the group's together, and often he literally isn't, he's like a ghost. Occasionally he makes his presence felt, turning up from his solo wanders with a generous offering; like putting a huge donut he's discovered on the table, slicing it up for us all or telling us he's discovered an internet café or good Wi-Fi spot. And this night I go to the bar to top my water bottle up, return and he's vanished.

'Sunny' Moh from Thailand is there in his place. She's small, pretty, full of life and has an infectious laugh that can be best described as a burst from a bubble gun of popping happiness bubbles. Moh is from a quite strict Muslim family and behaves at home, but as she works for our travel company, Intrepid (in Asia) she often gets the chance to break free of constricting religious beliefs, 'party Moh' then steps forth.

I'm enchanted by her beauty, laugh and love of life and she takes me off into dreamland when she tells me of her travels and her favourite place she's visited: this is a 'blue flame' volcano - there are only two in the world - on an island in Indonesia. They travelled up there through the night, saw the dance of the blue flame, watched one of the best sunrises she's ever witnessed and were able to walk around the rim. I try to impress her by telling her that in one of my fairytales I had a breed of wizards that were created, then at the end cremated (before shooting up into space as a blue star) by the blue magma of a special volcano and I never knew such a thing existed in real life. Moh gives a machine gun bubble laugh.

Around midnight I'm just about to climb on up the stairs to bed when I hear a cough on the steps that lead up to the door to the teahouse. Hard Easy Rider Dave is sat out there, smoking a roll up, African rap on his headphones, so he doesn't hear me when I say goodnight at first. I tap him on the shoulder and he jumps like a shell-shocked soldier. 'Hey dude.'

'Those mountains still have their heads hidden under grey blankets, sleeping?' I say, referring to the impenetrable grey mist that has fully descended into the valley again.

'Yeah, but tomorrow the sun will shine and they'll welcome us.'

'Yeah and if the sun shines we see Everest for the first time.'

'Dream on that dude.'

Left: Lukla. Above: Mani stones.

Namche Bazaar.

Sat April 25th 2015, Namche Bazaar, Nepal:

I only had a few hours sleep again. Still, I felt refreshed - my dizzy head cleared, appetite back - and excited about the day ahead, adrenalin fully pumping, but as I look out of the bedroom window I'm dismayed to see low grey cloud and sleet falling.

I mention the weather to Lalit at breakfast, he shakes his head. 'The conditions over the last few weeks are so wrong for this time of year, I see global warming effect more and more, something strange is happening.'

Diary entry:

This morning we set off for an acclimatization walk, high above Namche, trekking up over 1000ft. Up there you're supposed to get good views of the Himalayan giant mountains, including Everest for the first time, but the day was overcast, rain then snow fell, creating a grey foggy barrier, you couldn't see more than about 50ft in front of you, less than that in places.

A challenging walk up steep stone steps, over the tops, where it levelled out into spongy rolling grassland, scattered with wind bent small bushes. It looked and felt more like English *Wuthering Heights* moorland than the Himalayas, especially in the impenetrable mist and wet snow.

The wet steep steps on the descent were quite treacherous in parts. Then a figure like a ghost appeared out of the gloom, swaying and staggering up the steps, a Nepalese youth, rebellious look about him, in his leather jacket, a rebel that had cause to get into a fight, his head was badly gashed open, blood poured down his face. Lalit, Dr Mel and others in the group tried to give him assistance but he flatly refused, mumbling to Lalit that he been glassed in a fight but would be ok, then he drifted off up the steps and was soon a shadowy figure dissolving onto the gloom.

We then realised Rahul had drifted away like a ghost again. I was sure he was with us when we set off, but appeared to be struggling, perhaps he'd turned back? Lalit had to leave and go back up into the mist to search for him (other Sherpa guides were with us).

Having to carefully watch your footing going down - with people going at their own pace, but with a guide at the front and back - we became stretched out; I was part of the little group at the front. Near the base of the hill we passed a poor looking Nepalese family carrying fairly hefty loads in wicker baskets on their backs, a baby was in one.

Minutes later we arrived at the outskirts of Namche and began to walk down a passageway between two high stone buildings when….at first it sounded like the tarpaulin in the grounds of one building was flapping noisily in the wind, but a wind that wasn't there, all our puzzled attention was drawn to it. Then there was a rumble, and the ground began to shake.

'Earthquake, run!' shouted Mel.

Now the earth shook violently, it was like being on a cakewalk at a fairground and running the gauntlet at the same time: the two buildings above began to sway and crack, like paper being torn, rubble rained down, it seemed like in slow motion, a film scene. Luckily a small open camping field was directly ahead of us, but the stone side of the café/bar at the edge of this collapsed, a pile of boulders crashing like they were nothing more than sugar grains spilling out from a knocked over bowl (luckily no one was in there at the time).

The five or six of us in our little group, it's hard for me to recall who was there other than Mel and Lauren, were in a state of near collapse too, bending over, hands on knees, panting heavily, starring at each other with big wild eyes, many an expletive or Christian exclamation expelled. 'What the fuck, Jesus Christ, oh fuckin' god...'

Dust from rubble rose, confusion reigned, shouts and screams could be heard coming from down in the heart of Namche that was out of sight. Then our fear turned to concern for our friends, there was no sign of them behind us. Shouts were coming from behind those buildings, and anxiety rose as the damage to the building (the one on our left that we'd been passing) could be clearly seen; the front cracked, the far and rear sides partially collapsed. The one side that had remained intact was luckily the one we had passed by. Soldiers from a small nearby garrison rushed passed us heading that way, another with a huge automatic rifle stood on a small hill.

Several minutes of anxiety passed before Lalit and Sherpas lead the rest of our group to the safety of the camping ground. All except Rahul - not a great time to do his ghost busted act - and we prayed he'd returned to the teahouse earlier, but would he be safe there? How much damage had Namche suffered? Shouts, dog barks and alarms still rose up from the town over the hill.

We weren't allowed back into the town for half an hour or so. The word came up, there had been damage but not extensive, a few injuries, but we were warned the walk back to our teahouse - right over at the far side of the valley, situated at the top end of a slope - could be hazardous. This is the case, rubble and boulders are scattered on the steep steps down and all along the paths and passageways across town. Many stones have fallen from high walls above the paths on the right side, some of these walls are leaning over in parts. We keep to the left side as much as possible and tread carefully, legs stills shaking, fearing an aftershock.

At the top right of Namche there's a large hole in a guesthouse where the walls have fallen away. Round another bend we see the front third of an old, long, two-storey building is missing - like a knife has sliced through a colourless Battenberg cake, four hollow rooms stand exposed, a desk in one, and old computer monitor sat on top, next to the cutaway edge. No sign of people in any room, hoping they're all safe.

We all reach our teahouse safely – Rahul is outside and ok. But we are not allowed inside, it has suffered quake damage. Mel and Annabelle are led to one side by Lalit, they look ashen faced when he talks to them. Later, when the rest of the upstairs has been checked and given the all clear, we found out why they had a look of horror on their faces when we're taken, 2 by 2, to see the bedroom they shared. A pile of huge boulders has crashed through the ceiling and lie on their beds. If the quake had happened in the night or a few hours earlier or later they would have been killed or badly injured. A chill runs down everyone's spine. Young Annabelle breaks down in tears as the reality kicks in of the lucky escape. I put a comforting arm around her shoulder, inside I'm thinking 'count your blessings, a guardian angel is looking out for you,' but this is not the time to say that so I say nothing.

Shell shocked, we huddle back together in the dining area. In an attempt to show normal service is resumed a guide brings the menus around for lunch. Our appetites gone we order the quickest and simplest things. There's just enough water in the kettles for those who order herbal or standard tea or coffee. The water is off, but the quick thinking, resourceful Nepalese find a temporary solution, one after another they run off down to the Dudh Koshi River to fill up the sizable water containers on their backs.

The unity in our group may have become stronger but the happy holiday head has naturally dissolved. Now a collective consciousness dwells on being shaken to the core by experiencing the immense power of an angry Gaia, of chance, fate, luck, of what could have been and of the scale of the potential destruction out there. What's our next move? Lalit is the one we will have to turn to for answers to the latter.

He's out of the room for long periods of time, trying to make contact with people on the phone. When he returns, he momentarily stares glassy eyed before giving us the latest news: there's devastation in Kathmandu and other areas of Nepal, around 100 confirmed dead so far and an avalanche at Everest, 1 dead.

My mind goes back to that awful walk back from Hillsborough stadium on the afternoon of April 15th 1989. When we set off 6 were confirmed dead, by the time we reached the city centre 50 were dead. Same with the Boxing Day tsunami, not a major news story to begin with, a small number of deaths. I knew that if this was the death toll now, only a few hours after the earthquake, then the number of deaths would be much greater, it felt like ice water had been injected into my veins.

Then I noticed Lalit's eyes again, and several others in our group, staring into a black hole and the penny dreadful dropped. Lalit's family lived in Kathmandu, Aussie Paul's sister was a nun at Kopan monastery and his wife was staying with her before going off visiting various tourist attractions, Mel lived in the Kathmandu Valley and had friends there, Southern Paul knew people who were at Everest preparing to attempt a summit.

We all ask Lalit if his family are safe?

'My family are safe, but my house is cracked.'

Our meals and teas start to arrive, but few of us have much of an appetite and the food is picked at. My ginger, lemon and honey tea is kind of comforting in a small way, but I've only had a couple of sips, placed the cup back on the table, when I notice little ripples, then the dining room floor trembles beneath our feet. The first aftershock hits, a lot smaller than the major quake but still terrifying, we all bolt outside. It's over before we even get there, but we still remain outside for several minutes breathing heavily.

When we do go back in the dining room we stay there for the rest of the day. It becomes apparent that just about everyone else in the group has smartphones, and my failings at modern technology exposed, my proud Luddite stance foolish? All I'd brought with me was an old iPod mini and my 6-year-old (ancient in the fast changing tech world) simple, app-free mobile, all it can do is make calls, text and take a few photos, and I'd only left it with 70p credit on, I wasn't going to bring it at all. Later I will hear that the Chinese authorities located everyone stranded on their (or Tibet's I should say) side of Everest by picking up the signals of modern smartphones. This evening though, no one can get a Wi-Fi connection or contact the outside world with their expensive devices. When an internet connection is eventually working, the next day, Tom lends me the use of his smartphone to post a message on Facebook asking if someone will ring my family and let them know I'm safe.

In the evening, Nick, Scot's Dave, Stephanie, Lauren and me are gathered together on benches and chairs at the far end of one table. Lauren is sat between Nick and me and insists we squash up to her for warmth, it is a noticeably colder evening, but I think it's more of a stress relieving comfort huddle in the circumstances.

'Are you ok there?' Lauren asks me at one point when there is a lull in conversation, I've been rocking backwards and forwards. I laugh and explain I must have been regressing to infant childhood, as there is old family film footage of me as a baby, wrapped in a woollen comfort blanket, rocking away. 'You had me worried, thought you were picking up new tremors,' she smiles.

To pass the time we 5 take it in turns to tell of our top 5 favourite bands, albums, books and films. Then play a game wherein you have to tell two revealing truths about yourself and one lie, the others have to guess the lie. My 3 are: 1. I held up the start of the motorbike GP that had Barry Sheene on the grid. 2. I ended up with a groupie on the tour bus of indie rock band Killing Joke and 3. I ran the London Marathon in 3 hrs 10 minutes dressed as SpongeBob SquarePants. My mind wanders off into the future, if I'm ever playing this game with strangers again and I say I was stranded in a mountain village near Mt Everest after a major earthquake, would anyone believe that? I'm finding it hard to believe myself.

Later that night I step outside to join Hard Easy Rider Dave, Nick, Lauren and Scot's Dave, sat on the steps outside that lead up to the teahouse door, a couple of them are smoking a cigarette. If there was something a little more left-field on offer to smoke this night I reckon I would take a toke and inhale deeply down to my unsteady toes.

I glance up, at last a crystal clear night sky. I'm a stargazer, back home, when I take my dog for a pre-bedtime walk on the fairly light pollution free nature trail out the back of my home, I'll look up and marvel at the celestial nightscape, mighty Orion my favourite constellation. And here, high in the Himalayas, on following a brilliant white band - the heavens equivalent of Nepal's milky river, the Milky Way - I see Orion the hunter climbing above a mountain, the pulsing red light of Betelgeuse looking ready to explode at any minute.

A long outbuilding of the teahouse is obstructing the view, so I drift along the Milky Way a little way to get the full picture. Oh my, I'm breathless, the night art canvas before my eyes is one of the most beautiful I've ever seen. Up above, on full display in some of the clearest air on earth, a multitude of stars shine and twinkle like diamonds, falling down like fairy dust behind a jagged horizon; fresh snow covered majestic mountains fully revealed for the first time. Below these, looking like a Ladybird Book painting of nativity Bethlehem, the lights shine from the windows of buildings on the hillside of Namche, the cracks not visible at this distance in the dark.

I call everyone to share this vision - going inside to urge Annabelle and Chandler (sat deep in each other's company as usual, probably more so now, a close bond forever, after sharing this day's never to be forgotten experience) to come outside. They'll thank me for introducing them to this sweet Christmas carol card, an exquisite example of the beauty of planet Earth as you are likely to see, on this night of all nights, the end of a tragic day in history, the full scale of which is not yet known to us.

Over those pretty mountains, ghosts of the present are gathering. Over those pretty mountains down a deep valley, like a deep wound in the dark, a powerful presence looms, mighty shaken Everest broods. Crushed beneath her feet the casualties, dead and wounded of a battle man has lost to Mother Nature, smothered and broken by her weapons of war: snow, ice and rocks fashioned into a deadly tsunami, an avalanche that engulfed our dream destination, Everest Base Camp. The potential conquerors of the world's highest mountain again struck down, a battlefield of devastation: ripped, torn and buried tents amongst ripped, torn and buried bodies.

Heartbreak and heroes, a modern day Florence Nightingale - with exemplary medical skills and astonishing courage - crawling injured out of the avalanche, coming to the rescue of so many. It will be weeks later that I'll read of the heroics being performed by Brit, Dr Rachel Tullet, less than 20 miles away from my Christmas card scene. She helped save the lives of 23 critically injured people despite having a badly inured leg; torn ligaments, cracked patella, and had a gaping wound. At one point she was treating 30 people on stretchers, as well as certifying the dead and organizing all the patients to be carried down to another camp. The following day Tullet stitched up herself without anaesthetic.

Latest news: 600 dead in the earthquake.

I go up to bed around 10.45 pm. Everyone else has already turned in, all except Hard Easy Rider Dave who seems to sleep less than me. I've not been getting much sleep on the trip as it was, so don't fancy my chances of making it to a pleasant dreamland with my nerves on edge, lying in a bed yards away from another earthquake damaged room, strewn with boulders, aftershocks predicted and words that maybe weren't wise to part with this time from Lalit, the danger of there being a landslip from the hill above our teahouse.

Back home, on going to bed, I often listen to the radio, BBC 6 Music or my iPod in the dark. I'm someone who can drift off to sleep listening to music on headphones, even LOUD rock like Metallica, so I pull out my iPod from my rucksack in the hope it will do the trick tonight. The first track shuffle throws up is Graham Coxon's 'Freakin' Out,' I have to laugh inwardly at the freak chance of this being up first. I press skip, I need lullabies and calming sounds and know I've put plenty on my iPod to complement the landscapes I was heading for. Closing my eyes listening to First Aid Kit – 'Shattered and Hollow,' Kathryn Joseph - 'The Bird,' New Order – 'Truth,' Leftfield – 'Universal Everything,' Scarlet Chives – 'Hunting,' Cocteau Twins – 'Lazy Calm' and 'The Thinner the Air,' Laura Marling – 'Walk Alone,' and her version of 'Blues Run the Game,' Sharon Van Etten – 'Your Love Is Killing Me,' Fleet Foxes – 'Your Protector,' Madam - 'Fall On Your Knees,' Damien Jurado - 'Metallic Cloud,' PJ Harvey – 'Dear Darkness,' She Drew The Gun – 'If You Could See,' Duke Garwood – 'Heavy Love' and A Guy Called Gerald – 'Emotions Electric,' are apt but soothing as I try to place my head in my bed back in the safe East Midlands of England.

A memory comes back to me, an 'earthquake' that happened when in that English bed one night; a brief shudder, the mirror in the bathroom vibrated, being slightly scared and alarmed at the time (it terrified my sister Elaine who was down from Manchester staying at my mum's in the same village that night) even though it was only something like 3.5 on the Richter scale. It made me wonder how scary it would be being in a major earthquake, in those far off lands on fault lines.

By the time Massive Attacks 'Unfinished Sympathy' is drifting along in my head I'm almost halfway to dreamland, when my bed, then the room shakes and rumbles. Above the sound of music I can hear shouts, footsteps running down stairs. Scot's Dave (who I now share a room with) jumps out of bed and nudges me on my shoulder, panic in his eyes.

'I'm going nowhere,' I say with false bravado. 'I'm not running from this thing anymore, you can't escape fate and Mother Nature.'

Dave seems to agree, the aftershock has now passed, and climbs back into bed; soon he's asleep again, occasionally making a noise like a far off Yeti howl echoing out of the mountains. I eventually manage to get a little sleep but am awoken by an aftershock alarm call at 5.00 am, a small one this time.

I glance out of the bedroom windows, those pretty mountains are still on show, mist billows up out of the deep valley, again lovely to behold. I take a photo, put on my clothes and wander down the stairs and outside to the same spot I'd viewed the previous night's Christmas card, to take in this new landscape masterpiece. With blue skies showing above I half have a mind to trek on up to the Everest viewing spot, the mighty mother mountain might just be making an appearance at last. But realise it would be irresponsible to go off on my own at this time of the morning, what if a bigger aftershock hits? So I return to bed, and do manage another hour or so of sleep.

Sunday April 26th 2015, Namche Bazaar:
At breakfast Lalit gives us the latest sickening news: at least 2000 dead in the earthquake, including 17 dead at Everest Base Camp and over 60 injured there, the old parts of Kathmandu destroyed or badly damaged. He mentions those tangles of electrical wires I'd been so fascinated by in Kathmandu, they'd come down and electrocuted people in the streets.

As to our almost trivial situation, in comparison, there's no clearance from Intrepid to go on any further with the trek. Lalit had suggested we do this to give us a glimpse of the giants of the Himalayas. It is likely, though, that landslides have blocked both the paths we travelled up to Namche on and the one ahead. No one really has any heart to carry on now and when news comes that someone has died at Dingboche, one of the next villages along, we know the best thing is to stay put. As it turns out we're stranded here anyway.

There is some good news at last; Lalit secures a call for Paul to his wife and nun sister in Kathmandu. Both are safe, Kopan monastery has suffered damage but has largely withstood the major quake, all monks, the Lama and visitors there are uninjured too.

Outside we come across a local holy man sat in a lotus position, broad rimmed hat and robe draped around him, a little book open in front of him from which he reads prayers for the protection of our teahouse and us guests staying there. The owner of the teahouse, also wearing a broad rimmed hat, squats by his side, his wife comes over to us with offerings of tea and biscuits. I find this little ceremony deeply moving.

At first little groups of us or individuals wander off around Namche, but later well all join together to retrace our shaken steps to the scene of our ground zero; the little area we were passing when the big quake struck the previous day, wondering if there is any help that can be given.

On open grassland, in front of the half collapsed camp site building, temporary accommodation has gone up in the form of several tents to house those whose homes are too dangerous to live in at this present time, more are going up on the field we ran into after the quake. There a whole family cluster in and around a large tent; mum, dad, grandparents, little kids, still full of the joys of young life, running around playing with smiles on their faces, two dogs lounge in the sun, a chicken struts by, a little fire is cooking up lunch. Thankfully the sun shines this day.

We sit amongst the people in the first tent community mentioned, the owner of the campsite says he doubts any funding will reach this far out from Kathmandu. After about half an hour I go and wander around a little Buddhist garden adjacent to the open field. It is nice to have solitude for a while, running my hand down prayer wheels before walking clockwise around a cracked stupa. From there I go on up into the park and the Everest view point. There's quite a number of people here today, mainly tourists stuck in Namche, as the skies are clear, the sun shines and more of the larger mountains are on show, not yet the big boys and Mother Everest though. The grassy hill here is also obviously a safe spot to gather and while away the time.

Diary entry:
The cloud was lifting a little in the direction of the great mountain, a griffon vulture swooped down the valley, eager to join the feast ahead; along the line of the trail to Dingboche, a pack of the huge carrion eating birds circled. A Nepalese guy explained they were feeding on yaks that had been swept away to their deaths down the valley side by a landslip. A bloodcurdling sight, something I'd only seen before in films, I pray that yaks were all they were feeding on. I'd read up on griffon vultures when checking out the wildlife of the Himalayas before coming out here. They've developed a taste for human flesh, guests of honour at 'sky burials:' an old tradition practiced by the Vajrayana Buddhists. When people die, their bodies, deemed an empty vessel, the soul having moved on, are left out on mountain tops, exposed to the elements, given to nature, either to decompose or be fed on by birds of prey and other scavenging animals.

On three sides of the Everest viewing hill are deep, deep valleys. I stepped up onto a viewing platform. Way down at the bottom of one of these chasms, looking like Lilliput, a little village lay. My attention was drawn several hundred feet into the air above this hamlet, but still within the walls of the giant valley, yet another helicopter from Lukla was heading up to Everest to bring back the bodies and injured.

I started talking to a guy from London – late 50's, grey beard, glasses – lying on the grassy hill, alone save for his Sherpa guide, all his trekking gear spread around him. He explained he'd been on his way to Everest Base Camp with a group similar to us, but had started to suffer badly with acute mountain sickness, so had no option but to turn back and be helped down the trail by his Sherpa. His group had pressed on. Since the big quake he'd not been able to contact them and didn't know if they'd been caught up in the avalanche. Those worried, haunted eyes again.

I stared off down the valley, past the statue of Sherpa Tenzing, see strips of blue sky, dirty white clouds slowly parting like curtains. Some of the giant mountains took centre stage, a mere glimpse of the slopes of Everest, then the show was over, the curtain began to drop again, greyer clouds billowed up like smoke. I felt a pang of disappointment, this might have been my last chance to see the 'Holy Mother,' if, as likely, we can't go on nearer to base camp.

But selfish desire is put into perspective when you see vultures circling, rescue helicopters heading for Everest and then, a few moments later, the earth began to move violently again, this felt almost as strong as the major quake.* Even here on the this safe and solid hill top everything rumbled, shook and swayed from side to side, a couple of sturdy old trees looked like they were streamers blowing in the wind. On the mountain sides on the far side of the valleys, off to the right then left, there is a loud resounding crack, followed by a rumble and whoosh as ice and snow falls, and psychological ice falls down my spine, I shudder, scared, so very scared.

*We hear later it was around 6.9 on the Richter scale.

Shouts and alarms again rise up from Namche, my immediate thoughts are for the safety of my new friends, I tell the trekker from London. 'Go, go see if they're safe mate,' he says.

I run down the hill and am mightily relieved to see them grouped together in the same spot we gathered after the first big earthquake struck, 24 hours or so back. I learn that several of them had been helping shift boulders from the half collapsed camp site building and had to jump to safety. Some stay there for a while, others head back to the teahouse, I head back up to the Everest view point, I feel safe up there.

The temperature has noticeably dropped, I'm chilled to the bone. Soon most people leave the hill, all except the guy from London, who, at this point, had nowhere to go, his Sherpa guide had gone down into Namche when the aftershock hit to try and find him a room in a guesthouse. I stay with him to keep him company.

Earlier you could see down to the valley bottoms, now an eerie and impenetrable grey shroud surrounds us, 360 degrees, yet helicopter pilots somehow continue to negotiate their flying crafts back and forth to Everest, incredibly brave. Not that I can see them as I peer through the glassless, twisted window of a quake, half tumbled down, small building near the valley edge.

Another heart stopping crack up in a mountain, to the rear, as more ice, snow and rocks crashed down into the valley below. Prayer flags flap in the biting wind, ghost like wisps of mist drift up onto the hill and circle us, a rickety old wooden gate creaks on its rusty hinges, I'm frozen with cold and fear.

The London man's Sherpa returns, as ever with these fantastic people, he's put his own well-being aside to look out for the man in his care, he's found him a room.

'Do you need any help carrying any of your gear down?' I ask.

'No, just watch this little fucker go,' he replies.

The Sherpa smiles, in an instance he has gathered everything up and is heading off down the trail with it all on his back.

More tents are going up around the camp site area, not those of tourists, more Nepalese families have no option but to camp out for safety, many of their homes further cracked from the big aftershock. And as I tread carefully past the rubble back towards our teahouse, I step aside to let two groups of Nepalese carrying already fully erected large tents up the path. Over a fence on open ground in front of other buildings a long row of wooden temporary beds are lined up on the grass.

When I arrive back at the teahouse I'm informed we're moving to a more soundly built large guesthouse a short distance away. Apparently another major earthquake is being predicted, it could be over 8 on the Richter scale, possibly between 8.00 and 11.00pm that night.

I never learn where this information has come from or if it's an unwanted rumour that has spread like wild fire. We have no option to sit and wait anxiously for it to happen in the dining area of the new guesthouse. At this time on a Sunday back home, I'd be with friends in my local, having a laugh, pint in hand, in front of a real fire watching live football, I wanted an adventure.

There are a lot more trekkers in this big guesthouse, many are bringing down mattresses and blankets to sleep under tables for protection, some go down to the basement. Our group, gathered around tables in one corner, are surprisingly upbeat, even with touches of gallows humour, for a while. A Sherpa, with the steadiest of hands, is building a playing card Mount Everest. 'Who wants a bet that the quake hits and the cards fall just as he's about to reach the summit,' says Irish Tom.

But we're all wearing masks to hide our fear, the anxiety and tension builds and is palpable, helplessly waiting the arrival of another major earthquake. The only thing I could possibly compare it to is what the London families felt during the blitz of World War 2, awaiting the German bombers to arrive. The only difference being is that was almost a certainty for months on end, night after night in 1940, a cold clear fact, not rumour or in the unpredictable hands of Mother Nature. I realise this is just a tiny insight into the nerve shredding nightly fear they had to endure, but I now realise just how amazingly brave and stoical they were.

I look across to Southern Paul, he's started to shut down for long periods of time I've noticed, hunched over, eyes staring way off into the distance. This guy has four kids and it's obvious his thoughts are thousands of miles away with them and his wife, especially now we have passed into the doomsday prediction hours.

Around 10.00 pm we dive under tables when a tremor begins, this quickly passes however, the clock ticks excruciatingly slowly, round past 11.00pm. Yet the fear remains, Mother Nature doesn't run by man's clocks. Several of our group have decided to stay down in the dining room and sleep under tables too. I try to convince myself and others that the warning was just a stupid rumour, until someone points out that the second quake in New Zealand was bigger than the first, thanks.

Then there's one great stress relieving moment: Chandler goes up to his room, which he shares with fellow Canadian Nick, who had gone to bed early. As Chandler opens the door, Nick sits bolt upright, wild eyes and screams, then calms down and says: 'I'm always dreaming that people are trying to rob me.' Not 'oh fuck is there another earthquake.' Outside in the corridor a dozen nervous heads have popped out of their bedrooms in fear of what was going on.

Guess you had to be there, but when Chandler comes down stairs and recounts this to those of us who are still up, we are in absolute hysterics, tears of laughter, one of the best laughs I've had in ages, so weird how the human mind deals with situations. I go up to bed and inexplicably have the best stretch of sleep I've had on the entire trip so far, but this is still only about 3 hours in a row.

The sound of a helicopter hovering over Namche wakes me around 5.30 am. In the darkened room I reach into my backpack for my camera, turn it on under the sheets, and look back at the photographs of Kathmandu, that beautiful sunny day of April 22nd, taking me back amongst those temples and shrines, the magnificent ancient Durbar Square. But it's the faces of the people in the photos I linger on and am haunted by. For the first time maybe, it's not about the ever growing casualty numbers, I'm looking at Nepalese people who in all likelihood were in the same now devastated areas when the major quake struck: the holy man and his wife sat in their spot in an old temple, ready to give blessings to tourists, the old woman sat amongst the pigeons and the cow in Durbar Square, her pitiful amount of possessions around her. One photo I stare at longer than the others in the dark; the little boy in a little holy square, bucket in hand feeding the pigeons. Does he go there every day? Please let him be ok God, tears run down my cheeks.

I've now learned that it's 81 years since the last major earthquake hit Nepal, and I find it hard to comprehend that I should be here, 81 years of history: the rise and fall of kings, 10 years civil war, the communists Maoists taking control before a fragile democracy was established, Ghurkhas going off to fight bravely for the British in World War 2 (and many other wars up to Afghanistan), all the failed attempts to summit Everest until the success of Hillary and Tenzing on the eve of the Queen's Coronation back in 1953, all the successes and failures on Everest since, The Beatles, Hendrix and Pink Floyd sitting in Durbar Square in the 60's and 70's. All those events, all those years, weeks, days, tens of thousand of hours with the Earth spinning on and pushing up tectonic plates with force the world over but not here. And then little me, who only occasionally travels out of his village, very rarely leaves the country, walks into a major earthquake in Nepal within days of arrival. I'd already fallen in love with the country and people, only to experience the force that had ravaged large parts of it and killed thousands of its inhabitants. How many people out there amongst the billions have been in two separate disasters when they occurred like I have? I'm thinking.

Diary entry
Monday April 27th 2015:
So it has been confirmed this morning, not unexpectedly, that we will be trekking on no further, there's a chance we could be stranded in Namche for days. I ask Aussie Paul and Scot's Dave if they would like to join me in having a walk up into the hills and a little way along the trail towards Dingboche, I've observed this from the Everest view point hill and seen many a person walking along there. They agree, but as we are about to set off that way from Namche a Nepalese man stands in our way and warns us not to go that way in case of landslides, before telling us he's the man to go to if we need any tents or other provisions.

So we turn back and walk down the same passage we were walking down at 11.56 am on April 25th, between the two buildings – the one on the left now barely holding together after the big aftershock – onto

68

the camping ground, now full of tents. To the rear of this, past the little Buddhist garden is another path, so we decide on exploring this.

This path turns out to be an off the beaten track that leads to a drop off a cliff into one of the valleys; so vast we can't see the bottom, clouds float by below us. There's evidence of a rock fall on the far side. It's a stunning spot, secluded and peaceful – apart from the occasional helicopter still heading for Everest – so we sit here for half an hour or so, at last feeling relaxed, swapping idle chat.

On the way back we come across the rest of the group sat up at Everest view point. Again the clouds clear just enough to give a tantalising glimpse of the giants before pulling down the shutters. Still, the sun shines above us. Feeling exhausted and stressed, with little to do, many just lie back on the grass in the sun. I'm sat next to Southern Paul on a small grass bank facing the statue of Sherpa Tenzing. A Nepalese family are down there, they have a little boy, a tiny dynamo dynamite of energy and fun; he runs, jumps, tumbles and rolls in circles around Tenzing, before plonking himself down between Paul and me.

He looks up at Paul and smiles, who comes back to his old self, heart taken. The boy has enough grasp of English to converse with us, names are exchanged. I point to Tenzing and ask if he is his hero. He nods and smiles. 'Will you climb Everest one day?' He nods and smiles, and I've no doubt he will be up there on top of the world one day.

Paul shows him a way of flicking stones, this simple game is enough for tiny dynamite to be the happiest kid on Earth at that moment, Paul's smiles and laughs along with him as a stone hits the target. I show him how to football volley a stone, he picks this up in an instant too. 'GOAL' we both start shouting as the stone ball hits the back of the bush net. Then I attempt to show him how to do an overhead kick, only to hit Aussie Paul, the boy laughs and picks up a larger stone and does an overhead kick that's heading directly for the target down under too, Paul rolls aside. The boy then runs and jumps into Rahul's lap.

All the women are in love, give him hugs and we're heartbroken when his sister comes to take him away.

Again I'm the last one left up there, enjoying the solitude when it becomes nearly deserted. On walking back into town I come across two more Nepalese lads playing football at the side of a bar and join in, letting them score a few penalties past me. I find an internet café open in the narrow streets of the town and enter in; a computer is free, time to get another update message on Facebook for my family back home. This done I check the latest earthquake news on the BBC website; my soul is punctured and deflated again when I read about and see harrowing pictures of the full scale of the quake for the first time. Well over 3000 dead, thousands injured, entire villages wiped out near the epicentre, UNESCO world heritage sites destroyed, the struggle to get rescue teams and aid to those most in need. Before - with no access to the outside world - I'd been walking around in a surreal living nightmare, ready to wake up at any moment, now the tragedy is stark and real, the news of the world. As if to emphasize the point a little tremor shakes me wide awake.

United with the rest at the guesthouse, we order tea. I suggest we all ought to swap contact details in case we're helicoptered out and sent our separate ways home. Moments later Lalit bursts in: 'Helicopters coming, quick, pack up and be ready, jum jum' (the Nepalese for 'let's go' but sounds like 'jam jam').

'You're a prophet,' Stephanie says to me.

We're ready to go within 15 minutes. This time we don't have the guides around to carry our heavy rucksacks, so get an example of just what heavy work they do as we set off 200ft up the steep steps to the helicopter landing platform, this a small curved area made up of paved rocks with a massive drop over the far edge into the valley below.

By the time I struggle up the last of the steps, the first helicopter is touching down, its blades never stop swirling, pushing me stumbling back. Then, as the first of our group are rushed aboard by Lalit, 'jum jum' and it immediately takes off, the down force sends me tumbling backwards over small wall (good job it wasn't over the edge of the valley). Momentarily the copter dives out of sight before rising again and flying away at speed.

Soon another red and white helicopter arrives on the scene to evacuate the next half dozen in our group. Five minutes later a black helicopter lands for us last five to board. Chandler and Scot's Dave climb into the front. A Sherpa, Annabelle and me plonk down on our rucksacks in the rear; the back seats have been removed as these are the same helicopters that brought the dead and injured back from Everest.

A few minutes of panic ensues, as the Nepalese guides outside can't close the front or rear left side doors. Eventually the pilot himself has to step out of his craft to sort it out. I start perspiring as I'm thinking, what if a strong aftershock hits at this moment, the helicopter could topple off the edge and with no pilot aboard we'd spiral on down to our certain doom. There's relief all round as he quickly fixes the door problem, jumps back in, grabs the controls and without a moment's hesitation lifts the helicopter into the air before putting it into a - guts in the mouth - nosedive into the valley before levelling out.

Annabelle at my side gasps and sheds a few tears, I notice this on opening my eyes, I hold her hand tight; in truth I was probably grasping her hand tighter in fear than she was mine.

Soon, like all of us, she's enjoying this ultimate white knuckle thrill ride; no theme park will ever come up with anything to match this as we swoop down the valley. Annabelle is comfortable enough to start taking photos and points out to me a landslip down onto the trail we trekked up to Namche on from Lukla (was it really only days ago? It seems weeks back).

Darkness and mist creeping into the valley raise the fear factor but within minutes of taking off we're hovering above the landing strip at Lukla airport, a swirl of dust and paper and we touch down, ushered out at haste, stumble past luggage, then with great shock and a kick in the stomach, we see a line of bodies, wrapped up like mummies.

As on our first arrival at Lukla, locals gather outside the fence and look on. This time witnessing a far more dramatic and dark spectacle than foreign trekkers off on an exciting adventure in their backyard.

Rooms for us have been found in a fairly large guesthouse just off the main street through Lukla, this is as far as we can return until further notice. We've not long arrived when Phurba Sherpa - my Manchester United supporting friend - turns up: with not enough room for him in the helicopters he's run it from Namche to Lukla in three and a half hours to be with us and to be home, this is his village.

I say to Phurba I'd like to visit the football ground he's mentioned, perhaps have a kick about with a few of our lads and his. But he shakes his head sadly and informs me it is covered in the tents of those temporary homeless, and I feel an insensitive idiot. Lukla didn't look too bad on the surface, but many homes are damaged and cracked here too. The Everest Gold Cup was to take place in Lukla in May but has been cancelled too, Phurba tells me. My mind again flips momentarily back to the Hillsborough disaster, when the words of Liverpool's legend of a manager Bill Shankly became facile, 'football is not a matter of life and death, it's more important than that.' Phurba was also due to run a marathon from Everest Base Camp to Lukla, this too will not now happen. I'm sure Phurba will be able to take part in these sporting events that are so dear to his heart again one day, when like the club he supports, Manchester United after the Munich air disaster, and his people and country will rise phoenix like to become Nepal United once more.

All our Sherpa and Nepalese mountain lads are back with us, catering for our every need, thoughtful, courteous, kind, friendly, smiles on their faces, when their thoughts must be on their families and wanting to return home and be with them during their country's darkest hours. A cynical person could say they're just carrying on with the job they're getting paid for and looking for extra tips. But I know working, public service, false smiling faces and manners when I see them. These, like the majority of Nepalese people I've encountered, are genuine; we've all bonded with them and taken them to our hearts.

My admiration for the people of Nepal was growing by the hour before the earthquake struck. In its aftermath, the way they have nobly and bravely dealt with such adversity, unified, helped each other out and continued to show kindness, smiles and friendship to strangers, has left me feeling humbled. An everlasting bond and love and I feel privileged to have been in their company and see the strength and beauty of the human spirit - in good times and bad - that has restored my faith in humanity, if only the rest of humanity shared their faith.

And that word 'privilege.' In Britain we - even on council estates like the one I was brought up on - are born into privilege: free education, the greatest universities in the world, the chance to get on and earn enough money to live in relative luxury. And even if you go through hard times and become unemployed (a situation I've been in several times in my adult life) you still have access to secure accommodation, benefits, free medical care via the NHS. The Tories might be doing their damnedest to dissolve this fine example of Britain being a caring society that looks out for those in the time of need, but even then, we have clean running water, cheap food a plenty, living in a country free from the threat of devastating earthquakes, volcanoes, tornadoes or any of the wildest tantrums Mother Nature can throw.

The UK is in crisis only when snow falls about a foot high, rain floods a few homes, the wind blows around 70mph and knocks over trees and partially damages a few homes, leaves fall on the rail tracks, the fat cats in banks lose their multi million pound bonuses, youths riot because they don't have the must-have material possessions they think they need, MP's use their expenses to buy a duck house. Yes we occasionally have a major tragedy (I was present at one), but nothing to compare to the catastrophic natural disasters that smash other parts of the world, often third world countries. We may remain rich in monetary terms, in culture and history. But seem to be becoming poor in values, morals and manners.

Nepal is rich in history and scenic beauty too, but the evidence of the former has largely been wiped out and the access to the latter temporarily blocked. Both are necessary for Nepal to attract tourism and have an economy that can stabilise the country and give many the hope of a decent standard of living.

Yet the people of Nepal remain rich in spirit and the best traits of the human character. At Kopan Monastery and in teahouses I'll see the words of the Dalai Lama on display:

'We are visitors on this planet. We are here for one hundred years at the very most. During that period we must try to do something good, something useful, with our lives. If you contribute to other people's happiness, you will find the true meaning of life.'

'Right from the moment of our birth, we are under the care and kindness of our parents. Later, when we are sick and old, we are again dependent on the kindness of others. Since we are so dependent on others at the beginning and end of our lives, how could it be that we would neglect kindness towards others in the middle?'

Lovely, but I believe the Nepalese didn't need the wise words of a premier holy man, they already seem to have the values he talks of in abundance. What little they have they share, be it kindness, friendship, smiles, hospitality, shelter or food.

And when it comes to stoicism, bravery, strength and endurance, there is no doubt why, during the Anglo-Nepalese war 1814-16, the British were so impressed with the courage of the Ghurkhas that they moved quickly to have it written into the peace treaty to recruit them to fight for the British Army, something they have so valiantly done ever since.

The day before returning to Lukla I was standing near our ground zero, when a Nepalese man - who was now living in a tent with his family - started talking to me. He asked where I was from, when I said England, his face lit up, he shook my hand. 'I've trained with the Ghurkhas and the British paratroopers,' he said proudly with enthusiasm. And he was the one who shook my hand, it should have been the other way around.

*

My plan, my prize, after hopefully making it to Everest Base Camp and back, was going for several deserved pints back in my local in England (I'd given up drinking at Christmas to get fit for the trip). But our new guesthouse had a bar, we were all pretty traumatised, even if we didn't show it or want to, the bodies at Lukla airport further scarring our souls. So several of us took the opportunity to have a few stress relieving beers, 'Everest Beer,' a picture of the worlds highest mountain on the can; the only sight of it I was going to get, about 20 times over the next few days. One of the cans now sits on my shelves at home to remind me of the fact.

A number of Everest Beers and other alcoholic drinks of choice, hit the spot that night for us, smiles and good banter returned (although that is something that rarely left this sound set of people).

Scot's Dave starts to become romantically involved with 'Sunny' Moh. I've become fond of her friend Gae; we spend a few pleasant hours sharing knowledge of our respective countries, our support for Manchester United and love of ghost stories. I write down several classic books and films for her to check out, Gae is more informative about the Japanese ones she tells me about.

The things a sleep deprived, exhausted, shell shocked, alcohol twisted mind can conjure up: when I reach the door - wooden, with slats in one section - to our bedroom I'm convinced someone is in there playing hip hop music. Scot's Dave is still out sweet talking Moh. Hard Easy Rider Dave likes hip hop, has he gone into the wrong room, fallen asleep and locked himself in? I can't put the key in the big padlock, but when I do manage to it still won't open, there is a bolt on the other side. I peer through one of the slats and swear I see a shadow move by, the thumping beat continues. 'Dave, is that you in there?' I shout with a tap.

'You mean me dude?' A reply comes from my left, Hard Easy Rider's bandana and baseball cap covered head is looking in through the door from the balcony at the top of the stairs that lead to this floor of rooms. He'd positioned himself on a chair outside there (and this will remain his throne for the rest of the nights in Lukla).

'Oh, there you are, I reckon someone has locked themselves in my room, I can hear hip hop music.'

Dave comes strutting down the corridor ready to administer his old marine moves to my intruders. First he tries the key in the padlock and it opens with no problem for him, he rushes in. Moments later I hear the toilet flush. 'Just bad plumbing dude,' he says casually, walking back out of the bedroom and back to his perch. 'This is the real deal,' he says, with a gold teeth glinted smile, turning up his African hip hop.

I walk into the bathroom, in need of a piss, flush the toilet, the hip hop sounds emanating from the pipes and cistern kick off again.

I'll have more problems caused by the door locking system the next morning. I go down to breakfast - taking the only key to the room - and push across the bolt outside the door assuming it is connected to the one inside. Dave is late and misses his breakfast.

'Ya locked ma in ya dick,' he says to me grumpily. 'Dick' he repeats several times, until I point out that it is a bit of a crazy door securing set up. If they have bolts on the outside then anyone can come along and lock you into your own room. If a military coup kicks off or the manager of the hotel flips out and wants to hold us all to ransom then the rooms are ready made cells, the hotel a prison.

Everest Beer helped me sleep at least, for around three and a half hours this time. I think I was awoken by an aftershock, but I'm not sure if it's just my shaken imagination anymore.

Tues April 28th 2015, Lukla, Nepal:
On an early morning pre breakfast stroll through Lukla I see a big sign near the airport, showing a map of the local attractions: a monastery down in the valley, shrines and mani stones up the valley and the chance of seeing red pandas in the woods. I consider checking out one of these activities later but by the time I'm

sat back in the dining room awaiting breakfast with the others, the unseasonable weather has scuppered my plans, this time it's full on monsoon rain.

I look down the main street of Lukla from the windows, amused by the antics of the street dogs. One shaggy white mutt sits on a concrete step in front of a shop, keeping an eye on his manor. If any bitch wanders by he makes advances, is visited by his hoodlum hounds, makes sure any rivals pay their respect on passing through, usually a good sniff will do, until a tiny little tearaway walks on by and dares to snap and yap cheekily in his direction. Shaggy launches himself off his perch and goes and bites the little dog on the bum to see him off.

Then the sadness and realisation of why I'm stuck in this Himalayan village sinks in. In the distance I spot an old man, sat on another step in front of a building: old boots, ragged clothes, a hood of a dirty coat the only protection against the rain, a few metal dishes and a bundle of belongings at his side. He's hunched up, not moving, as lifeless as a Guy Fawkes straw filled rag doll thrown onto a bonfire. Across from him on wasteland are a cluster of families, lucky to have an increasingly scarce tent; they huddle under these or tarpaulin from the rain. The children, as ever, pay no heed to being temporary homeless or the rain, and play on happily. And the sickness I feel is not just from a hangover. Here I am waiting to be served breakfast within four solid walls, still the privileged, above them in their own village. There's room at the inn, why aren't they given shelter? Then again they're so proud they'd probably turn it down.

Lalit gives us the latest news: near 4000 dead, talk of unrest on the streets of Kathmandu. And if this cloud and rain sets in for the day there'll be no flights, other than emergency rescue helicopters, in or out of Lukla today. We see one of the latter, a big Indian military helicopter coming into land. Smaller ones head up the valley, back to Everest and far flung corners of Nepal; isolated communities devastated and in desperate need of aid.

Feeling useless and helpless we all stay hanging around the dining room for a few hours in the morning, it's one of the rare times we are all together now. I look across to Chandler, even he doesn't seem his usual bubbly self now; quiet, almost sickly looking and sat on his own. Annabelle is another corner, away from him, and I wonder if they've fallen out. Then notice she's on her phone and it sounds like she's received a call from her Swedish boyfriend. After this she sits there checking messages on her smartphone. There's a commotion back to my left, Chandler has half collapsed, people pull him back onto a bench and lie him down, but the concern grows, he's struggling for breath, looking in a distressed state, close to passing out.

'Annabelle!' I shout and nod to where Chandler is, but she doesn't spot him at first or what's going on, thinking I'm gesturing to the large Indian helicopter taking off outside the window and goes to sit back down. 'No, Chandler,' I point his way. Now she looks sickly pale too as she rushes over, holds his hand as at first Nepalese try to give him medical attention.

They do their best but luckily we have Dr Mel in our group, she's just left the room but is rushed back. Thank god she is there and she immediately goes into doctor mode giving top medical care to Chandler; a quick examination of his symptoms, has pillows brought to be piled at the back of his head, asks him a few questions he whispers replies to, and administers any medicines needed, has an oxygen tank brought to him by one of our Sherpas, then arranges for him to be taken to the small Lukla hospital. Annabelle goes with them.

The diagnosis we later get, is that he has a touch of pneumonia, and has suffered from it before. You'd never have guessed, so young and fit, all the trip long. We're so happy and relieved to see him return later in the day, well on his way to a recovery, if not quite his old self. Annabelle rarely leaves his side for the rest of the trip.

Later an elderly American guy happens to come to our guesthouse, with a few younger Nepalese people. They work at Lukla hospital and are collecting funds for it as it's been damaged by the earthquake, we're happy to give what rupees we have spare.

Into the afternoon, and it's confirmed we're not leaving Lukla this day, the rain continues to fall, depression kicking back in after another dramatic and sad morning. The two Englishmen, an Irishman and Scotsman turn to our historic way of dealing or not dealing with problems in life, we go drown our selfish sorrows, it's unanimously agreed on between us, time to hit the Irish bar.

Who are we kidding when we tell ourselves we're just casing the joint out for the rest and just order a round of Irish coffees? A second round shortly follows as we play pool. White Russians are lined up next, as Aussie Paul arrives to join us; we're becoming comfortably numb and distant from the harsh reality out there in Nepal, and our inability to be able to do anything about the situation. Familiar western rock music booms out of the jukebox, a replica Irish bar of any town, bonding with lads, it's easy to imagine I'm out on the town a few miles from home on a Friday night.

But in one corner is a TV showing CNN rolling news: reporters at the heart of the worst areas of quake hit Nepal, then a good news story of someone people pulled alive from the rubble. The other clientele in the bar are far more bohemian looking than I'd get in any town close to where I live: also bedraggled, bearded and trek booted. And it's hard to avert your eyes from the walls and ceiling that are covered in Everest or bust graffiti and messages: 'Everest Base Camp to Lukla in 1 and a half days, record holders,' it says in black marker on the ceiling above my head.

Then it's back on the local brew, Everest Beer, as Moh and Gae turn up. Time for Muslim Moh to swap heads for Party Moh and let her hair down, Gae doesn't drink so stays sweet, shy and dry.

Around teatime our Sherpas suddenly turn up, they've tracked us down and brought the guesthouse menu with them so we can order meals and they can rush back and get them prepared for us. After briefly calling back at the guesthouse for the evening meal we head back out; to the 'Scot's bar' this time. I bump into a couple of guys from Yorkshire that I'd not seen since we were trekking on up to Namche before the big quake. We shake hands, happy to see each other safe and well. They introduce me to a couple of women from Manchester, one of these tells me she's been on BBC Manchester evening news. There's a good chance my sister will have seen this I say and it feels a strange scenario all round.

Southern Paul is on a mission to get pissed and block all the shit out, he's badly missing his wife and four kids now, showing us pictures of them earlier, emotion and pride in his voice. But when he lines up the tequila shots on the bar for us all, I know it's time to make my exit. My urge to do this is reinforced when a big guy from New Zealand - of Asian descent, he looks like a 6ft 5 Bruce Lee but without the legend's wisdom and self control - punches the ceiling and breaks a light ('boards don't hit back'). Others look on edge. There's a lot of pent up tension, trauma, and frustration bubbling below the surface, a spark like the one he's just let fly could release it all in an ugly way. A couple of our Nepalese guides are in here, not drinking, and they look on bemused, calm.

Back at the guesthouse I'm talking to Hard Easy Rider Dave, sat in his adopted spot on the balcony chair. This time he doesn't need his hip hop on as similar sounds and techno boom up from the bar below. He tells me of his new plans.

'The Camino Way dude, mission on, now I do it both ways to raise money for Nepal.'

I'm suitably impressed. 'Brilliant idea, a better script than the Martin Sheen film.'

'I'm thinking of having a t-shirt done 'Quake Survivor - Nepal 2015.''

I'm not sure about that, but his heart is always in the right place.

'And a tattoo with the same.'

Our conversation is interrupted by drunken voices coming up the steps, a near legless Southern Paul being escorted to his room by Irish Tom and an amused Gyaljen Sherpa. Earlier he'd fallen down the steps of the Scot's bar.

'I bet you thought your work carrying heavy luggage for us was done,' I say to Gyaljen, who laughs.

Wed April 29th 2015, Lukla, Nepal:
Diary entry.
The death toll is now approaching 5000.
Lalit informs us a new crack has appeared in the already weakened runway at Kathmandu airport; either caused by another larger aftershock or a stress fracture from the giant cargo planes coming into land with earthquake aid and rescue teams. In any event we will not be flying back there today.

I've mixed feelings on this. Part of me is dreading going back to Kathmandu and seeing the heartbreaking destruction and the plight of the people, if there is nothing we can do to help. Wishing we could leave the country via India. But the balance is tipped to the side of my brain that insists I must go back; Kathmandu enlightened me, lifted my soul, I'm part of this, forever, I can't turn my back on the city and its people now it's down on its knees. Maybe there will be British representatives and aid charities at the airport, I could let them know I'm willing to help in someway?

I was talking to a group of independent British Everest trekkers staying in the same guesthouse as us. They told me they'd been in touch with the British government and were informed of the possibility of stranded British citizens being flown into India on an army Chinook helicopter. Can't say this sat comfortably with me. I wasn't now entirely sure it had been right on our travel company's part, Intrepid, to rush us up to helicopters - at short notice - to fly us out of Namche, where we felt quite safe and were willing to wait to walk it back down to Lukla. Guess they were looking out for our best interests (they didn't pay for the helicopters, though, we had to) or maybe they just felt they'd be culpable if anything happened to us? But I've since read online, via someone's smartphone, that helicopters are scarce and valuable to the aid and rescue effort. I know the ones we were evacuated in had been involved in that. So certainly didn't want to use up the fuel, time and space of a mighty Chinook, and that of the soldiers who operated them, when they could be put to much more use helping those in desperate need. I'll get home in time enough, I'm sure.

I wander down the main street of Lukla, it's good to see the shops open and trading. I buy a couple of small prayers wheels and flags - to hang on the tree back home that I'd planted in memory of my dad, who we lost to cancer.

Coming out of the shop I bump into Thai ladies Moh and Gae, and join them walking around Lukla. Near the far end of the village we come across a little ceremony going on: a makeshift place of worship has been constructed out of a few large pieces of tarpaulin. Inside Buddhist icons have been placed, candles flicker, adult monks in their robes sit at the entrance to this, a few child monks congregate before them. Across from these a group of sombre looking villages sit on seats, an old woman in more traditional dress, her careworn, lined face full of character, now looks cracked with emotion, two sad eyes peer out.

Gae asks a Nepalese man what is going on and he whispers that it is a service for a local 17-year-old lad who was killed in the earthquake. We feel we're being intrusive and begin to walk away, but a woman with a big kettle of fruit tea comes over, offers us a cup each and says we're welcome to stay and pay our respects. It's impossible not for the tears to well up, my heart to hurt.

We return to the guesthouse, nearly everyone is there, in the dining room. This has a decent library of books in one corner: Everest expeditions, the history of Nepal, the origins of Buddhism and Hinduism in the country. A few of the group are sat reading these at tables, Mel, Irish Tom and Aussie Paul. I don't see Rahul, look out of a window, look back and jump as he has appeared out of nowhere again, another large donut for us all and a verbal map of the current best Wi-Fi connection. It's good to see Chandler looking well and he's busy scribbling away in an A4 notepad inventing a word game for us to play and kill time. Annabelle is by his side. Scot's Dave is all smiles with 'Sunny 'Moh' in a corner. Gae sat a little apart checking her smartphone. Nick, Southern Paul and Steph are chatting away, Lauren's writing in her diary. Hard Easy Rider Dave, full of crazy energy as usual, buzzes around all of us. For one of the last times the 15 are united in a way we were before the quake struck.

Many of the Sherpas are here with us too, plus a friend of theirs from Lukla they've met back up with, a shout goes up, 'Manchester!' I look around. 'Liverpool.' The young Nepalese guy who supports United's rivals, the one I'd encountered working behind the bar in Lukla at the start of the trek, has remembered me, a big smile on his face. 'Your team lost at the weekend, we catch you.'

'They did?'

'Yes,' he laughs.

Lalit comes in from making the never ending series of phone calls. 'Good news, we have a flight tomorrow morning, first south to near the border with India, then back to Kathmandu.'

There are just nods of acknowledgment for the same shared reason I outlined earlier, plus apprehension at going back to a badly damaged city with the omnipresent threat of more aftershocks or another big quake inflicting more destruction.

'Are we going to be staying in Kathmandu Guesthouse again?' asks Nick.

'No, the Thamel district badly damaged, many deaths there, an overhanging wall next to the drive up to the guesthouse could come down at any time. You'll be staying in the grounds of a hotel in the northern suburbs,' Lalit explains.

'What about the belongings we left in lock ups at the hotel? My passport is there,' says Scot's Dave.

Chandler has left hundreds of pounds worth of electrical equipment there.

'Don't worry they all be collected and brought to you.'

We're all satisfied with these arrangements; it's out of our hands, just another unpredictable instalment of our steps back home.

Lalit's face brightens as he notices a Nepalese man enter the dining room, he calls him over. He's a Sherpa with a weather-beaten, leathery face with different shades of brown and olive, an unkempt black beard, purposeful eyes, an aura of adventure about him. Lalit shakes his hand with reverence, as he introduces him to us.

'This is Yeti, he summit Everest six times,' Lalit holds up six fingers as if to emphasize the point.

'Wow – six times! – fantastic,' come the replies, as we gather around.

Yeti gives a modest smile.

Lalit tells us how he recommended 'Yeti' to British business friends that own a flag making firm. For the last two years Yeti had been commissioned to lead a team to the summit of Everest for the perfect ad picture; one of their flags on top of the highest mountain in the world. The mission has been cancelled for the last two years, first after the avalanche of 2014 and now postponed again after the quake avalanche this year. British business empire flags days will have to wait, the only flags that belong on Everest this season are prayer ones.

After Yeti leaves the conversation stays centred around Everest. A top Sherpa climber can earn around $3000 if he summits, a life changing amount to them, but there's the high risk of a heavier price to pay if things go badly wrong. 16 Sherpas were killed in the avalanche of 2014, and it's reported many have been killed in this quake avalanche [10 at the last count].

Over the years over 250 people have died trying to climb Everest. Southern Paul, Irish Tom, Aussie Paul and me discuss one of the most haunting and controversial deaths, that of one of the most recent of British climbers to die on Everest (in 2006), after a brave, if foolhardy summit. David Sharp made a solo attempt to climb Everest using no oxygen, Sherpa guides or radio contact. It is presumed he made the summit. On his descent, probably suffering from exhaustion and hypothermia on one of the coldest nights of the year, he took shelter in a rock overhang called 'Green Boots Cave,' named after the green booted body lying at his side; that of Indian climber Tsewang Paljor, who had died 10 years earlier in 1996. David Sharp sat there for many hours, arms clasped around his knees. Around 40 climbers passed him but none came to his assistance.

Everest legend Sir Edmund Hillary poured down criticism and scorn on those who refused to help. 'I think the whole attitude towards climbing Mount Everest has become rather horrifying. People just want to get to the top. It was wrong if there was a man suffering altitude problems and was huddled under a rock, just to lift your hat, say good morning and pass on by. Callous climbers don't give a damn for anybody else who may be in distress and it doesn't impress me at all that they leave someone lying under a rock to die.'

Yet despite all the loss of life and considerable risk, hundreds of climbers are drawn to take on Everest each year, the great must-have adventure badge, an obsession. And even little old simple adventurer me has now felt a semblance of the Everest Death Star magnetic pull. My personal expedition was to make it to Base Camp, to see the great mountain, and as I didn't achieve either, I am almost consumed at times with the thought of returning. Everest lures me back, even to Base Camp where around 40 people have died in the last two years, in this month, April.

The talk of Sir Edmund Hillary had made Lalit's ears prick up. 'He's like a god around here, a god. He changed our lives, created everything, the Everest industry, funded schools and hospitals, even Lukla airport you flew into, his foundation built that. We used to have nothing; poor people had to walk many miles out of the mountains down into the valleys to work on farms to survive. Now we have hope, of a better future, even things like clean running water he put in place, the man is up there with Everest.'

*By chance Peter Hillary and Jamling Tenzing Norgay, the sons of the first men to summit Everest, were both leading separate trekking parties near Everest when the earthquake struck. Then they bumped into each other in a tea-shop in Tengboche.

*

After tea all but Aussie Paul and me plug themselves into their smartphones for a while, then we fracture into separate groups or solo wanderers. My Everest Base Camp trek adrenalin has long since drained away, replaced by spells of sadness, beer poison, not eating well, cabin fever, aftershock nerve shredded, and lack of sleep; fatigue finally kicks in.

I go up to our room to try and have a nap, close the curtains, turn out the light, put on my iPod to shut everything out and try and relax, but my mind trips out, a black magic lantern of images at stop frame animation speed. The bedroom shakes a little and I don't even know if it was a real small aftershock or I'm fucking imagining them anymore. The plumbing starts performing hip hop again: the bathrooms are curiously constructed, maybe it's for anti condensation ventilation but they left a half a foot gap on the top of the concrete walls that separate our bathroom from the ones for rooms either side. You can hear anyone who comes in those over each side, even voices from bedrooms; some Russian raised voices drift up from the one to the right, someone splashes about in the sink to the left, laughing at something said by someone back in the bedroom.

I give up trying to sleep, read *To Kill a Mockingbird* for a while (Boo Radley you can't scare me now), then open up my notepad and write a little about the last few days experiences (I'd started a journal as soon as I booked my trip back in January, and having had my autobiography published I have kept a diary ever since. Writing started out as a kind of therapy, the first thing I ever wrote was the Hillsborough chapter from *If the Kids are United*, I needed to get it out of my system, it helped me deal with being at the tragedy).

After I've done this, all goes quiet, steady and still for a while, my eyelids droop, dream cinema reels begin to spin, was I really with a female friend and our dogs walking in English countryside, bluebells singing, bring it back…the boom beat and rap of hip hop slaps me awake. I run to the toilet to kick the cistern, then realise it's real music coming from outside. I pop my head out the door; Hard Easy Rider Dave is sat on his balcony perch, African rap blasting out. Oh fuck it, might as well join him.

'What's up dude, you looked washed out,' Dave says on seeing me slump down on the balcony floor in front of him.

'Just tired and hungry, but I'll survive.'

'You fancy a burger?'

I'd been vegetarian since arriving in Nepal, this was recommended on TripAdvisor, to avoid a dodgy stomach, especially up in the Himalayas as much of the meat has to be carried all the way up from Lukla. Like the prize of me having a pint back home in my local pub in England after making it to Everest and back, I was going to wait until the Burger King at Doha airport to have a meat feast again.

'Hmm not sure, sounds like we've a lot of turbulent flying to do tomorrow, don't want a dodgy stomach for that.'

'Nah dude, the meat is fine down here, the burgers in this internet café down the way are top dollar, I've had one, Nick's had one….'

He goes and knocks on the adjacent bedroom door of Nick's, who must be in there having nap too; a quick shout of fear goes up, before there is a shuffle across the room, and the unbolting of the door, Nick's tired, fearful eyes appear.

'The burger dude, tell Tony how great they are.'

'Yeah great,' replies Nick quietly, before disappearing back inside.

'Ok, sounds good to me,' I say.

The internet café that had these burgers on offer was quite plush, it wouldn't look out of place in any town or city in the UK. And Dave was right, the burger was very tasty, melted in my mouth, so did the carrot cake, washed down with coke, served by polite Nepalese staff. But the clientele left something to be desired, in fact several fuckin' infuriated me: trekkers and adventurers from certain countries, who half threw a hissy fit. First because they'd had to wait more than five minutes for some food, but mainly because the Wi-Fi was down. One slammed his coffee down on the table and sulked, another demanded: 'Why man, why is the Wi-Fi down?'

Hmm not sure dude, maybe it's because you're in a third world country in the middle of one of the biggest natural disasters and tragedies in their history. And I feel proud to be a smartphone dunce Luddite again. These people weren't crying because they urgently needed to contact home to let loved ones know they were safe, they'd have done that by now, no, they were having serious tech withdrawal symptoms, the Borg Collective unplugged for 5 minutes and they couldn't handle it. I remembered going down on the train to London the previous autumn, loving watching the world go by outside the carriage windows, hoping to get into entertaining conversation with a stranger, but every other person on the carriage had their heads lost in cyberspace. In this environment, in the circumstances, I found that addiction and rudeness to local people hard to stomach.

At least Hard Easy Rider Dave's foray onto the world web had some substance to it at this moment; he showed the messages of support and promises of donations starting to come in for his walking the Camino Way for Nepal quest he was planning. My taste buds treated, I had to get out of there, though.

*

Most of the group hung around the dining room in the evening for a while, then turned in early again, with the flight out of Lukla, south to Biratnagar taking off about 6.00am. This left the night hawks Hard Easy Rider Dave and me the only two up and about after 10.00pm again, perched on the balcony, music started to boom out from the bar below.

'Fancy a beer or two down there dude?' Dave asked.

'Not sure, my stomach feels sound enough and filled for the flight, don't want a hangover to fuck it up.'

'Just a couple man, I'll get them in.'

'Ok.'

We enter into the dark and sleazy does it bar, western rock posters adorn the wall: The Doors, Hendrix, The Beatles, Nirvana. Psychedelic disco lights circle the room or pulse in the hazy smoke, drifting up from a large Arabian looking water pipe on the bar being shared by local youths sat there, others play pool. The DJ puts on one of my favourite tracks, Hendrix's 'Purple Haze' followed up by Coldplay, some Nepal rock pop, techno and ambient, then George Ezra's 'Budapest,' [which my mind has chosen for the track that will always throw me back into that bar that night].

I feel in my element as we knock back a few Everest Beers in a barely lit alcove in a far corner. Dave, however, is fed up they've not yet played any hip hop. So, shortly after three beautiful and sexy Scandinavian blonde women have entered the bar and started to play pool with captivated Nepalese youths, he suddenly takes music matters into his own hand, exploding into an improvised rap. You would have had to have been a touch typist extraordinaire or shorthand master on speed to have gotten his hyper lyrics down. All I can say is, they veered from a quake aborted Everest trek to having sex with hot Swedish women over a pool table. With his hands jerkily throwing black rap art moves and Dave's head thrusting towards me in and out of the dark, psychedelic lights dancing on his face, The Doors 'The End,' on in the background, I think I'm on a LSD trip into *Apocalypse Now* (just need the sound of a helicopter taking off from Lukla) or a David Lynch film, and I have Dennis Hopper losing it next to me. All I can do is laugh manically.

I get one more round of Everest in. The guy behind the bar offers me a marker and asks if we would like to leave a message with the rest on boards behind our seat in the corner.

Dave puts his favourite new moniker 'Quake Survivor, Nepal 2015.' I put my name, county, country and '29/4/2015 Quake week, RIP the many.'

We're out of there by about 12.00 am, but the bar is below the bedroom I share with Scot's Dave, and booms out music until the early hours. Dave in the bed at the side of me sleeps through all this as usual. Why can everyone else in the group - apart from Hard Easy Rider - sleep through everything? I heard some say they'd had over 8 hours some nights. Guess they're worn out physically and emotionally, but I

81

am too and still lie wide awake for hours at a time, even after several Everest Beers. Then the obligatory night tremor puts the nerves on edge, seconds of fearing is it going to get stronger? Was it strong enough to topple already damaged buildings or ground planes again?

Thurs April 30th 2015 Lukla to Kathmandu:
I was probably the last one to bed and I'm the first one to rise (although I wouldn't be surprised if Hard Easy Rider Dave spent the entire night sat on his balcony perch). At 5.00 am I wander down to the guesthouse courtyard, it's a sunny, clear beautiful morning at last. Up above Lukla the snowy mountains look magnificent, and I realise that if this is the scene at Lukla, the lowest place on the trek we were to go on, just how incredible the views would have been higher up if the climate change messed up weather hadn't been persistent in grey washing out the landscapes. But it's not a time to feel cheated after the disastrous events of April 25th.

Chaos ensues at Lukla airport. In *The World's Most Extreme: Runways*, it showed just what a difficult job the lone traffic controller has here at the best of times, with passenger flights full of Everest adventurers and climbers, plus all goods, being helicoptered in. Now he has to balance the erratic timetable of flights taking out the mass of travellers desperate to leave, more essential goods coming in and rescue helicopters landing and taking off.

Inside the departure lounge the staff of Lukla also have to work hard to try and get everything running smoothly. And their jobs - and our trek leader Lalit's - are not made any easier by idiots like me losing their boarding cards 10 minutes after being issued with one. I'd gone over to the counter of souvenirs on spotting a postcard of the Kumari; you couldn't take a picture of the little living goddess of course, so this would be a fine reminder of the moments I was lucky enough to be in her presence. I either left the boarding pass on the counter or stuffed it into the hidden depths of my big rucksack.

Lalit kept his cool, just about. 'Jum jum' he shouted to me when I stood there like a lemon when the rest of our group were called forward to hurry onto the plane. He still found a way of getting me on board and didn't even kick me up the arse when he should have done.

Last onto the Yeti Airplane I sat on a seat right at the back, the dunce in the corner. After welcoming us all aboard with a sweet smile and a 'Namaste' and offering us all Yeti Airline sweets, the stewardess sat next to me. I smiled and said 'hello,' and asked if her family were ok?

'Yes thank you, but house in a bad way, so much damage in Kathmandu and....so sad,' her stewardess mask fell and tears seeped out of the corner of her eyes.

'I'm sorry,' was all I could say in return.

As the Himalayas were left behind and we headed into southern Nepal, the landscape below became green and fertile, with gently rolling hills and the occasional rural village; no sign of damage from up above and it almost had the look of the English countryside to it. It's not long before we touch down on a small runway, surrounding by fields of tall grass blowing gently in the warm breeze, near the town of Biratnagar. We walk down the steps onto a baking, hazy runway, under a hot sun, our mountain layers are soon shed, down to t-shirts and light tops. India is only a walk away, I've always wanted to visit there and wish I could just walk across those fields of grass into the country. None of us venture anywhere other than parking our bums on rows of aluminium benches in a more orderly departure hall for an hour, apprehensive about our return to Nepal's capital.

It seems most people from Lukla are taking this diversion back to Kathmandu, as by chance, sat at my right, are the 3 Swedish women who were in the bar the night before. I'm hoping Hard Easy Rider Dave doesn't notice and come over to serenade them with the rap track he so stylishly included them in.

*

The small plane disappears back into one of those towering turbulent clouds. I'm no longer scared of flying, it's being down on unstable ground that I worry about now. A sharp intake of breath, anticipating what's down there, as we drop back out of the cloud; the outer reaches of Kathmandu hang precariously onto steep hillsides amongst terraced fields.

On flying down over the city itself I don't see the mass destruction I feared. Then realise this is a huge city with a population of over a million, if it had been nearly wiped out the disaster would have been apocalyptic in scale. What you do see however is evidence that many buildings and homes are sufficiently enough damaged for them to be uninhabitable, or now in a fragile state that could collapse if another big aftershock or quake hits - and the daily rumbling of the Earth gives constant threat of that: tents are everywhere, football pitch size groupings of them in places. It's like flying over a big music festival.

Kathmandu airport is a hub of earthquake aid and rescue activity, plus foreigners fleeing a disaster zone, aid workers, the world's media and Nepalese - who'd fled the nest at some time in their life or recently - returning home in their country's and family's time of need and sorrow. There's also a United Nations of army personnel. Huge cargo planes from a variety of countries, helicopters of various size; military, rescue and civilian. Groups - and snaking lines - of people as busy as an ants nest. Piles (although nowhere near enough) of earthquake relief essential items: food, medicines and tents, ready to be distributed to fallen communities of Nepal.

The shuttle bus takes us to a smaller arrivals lounge than the 'international' one. We're quickly processed and herded outside to a temporary luggage carousel, a scramble as the bags arrive, then onto taxis in groups of 6, off into the suburbs of Kathmandu, a city the focus of the world right now. And yet, at first, on the surface, you feel relief that utter destruction doesn't meet your eyes. In fact - if for some inexplicable reason you were here without seeing any news - for sizable stretches along the main road and streets from the airport you wouldn't know there'd been a major earthquake; other than areas of people living in tumbledown houses on rubbish and rubble strewn areas of wasteland, that you could attribute to an earthquake, but are the same visions of a third world existence that had met my eyes on arriving here on April 21st.

Then you'll suddenly come across a scene from the blitz: a small group of buildings collapsed, ones half standing, hollowed out, like an old dirty doll's house on a rubbish tip that's had its hinged front yanked off, to reveal the rooms within open to the elements, scattered and ruined; a double bed hangs vertically (kept in place by a few jammed bricks) lengthways down the front of the building, people with hollow eyes stare up. Smoke rises from a mass of cremations down by the river.

Further along are more temporary tent communities. Then, looming up above the street, is an ancient temple tower, the pagoda top section twisted and hanging down at an angle on fallen bricks, like an infant giant has reached down and bashed his Lego tower. Around another corner a group of people are gathered, animated gestures and a few raised voices in response to the man who is addressing them. 'They're complaining about the lack of aid and being given dirty fuel for their vehicles,' our driver explains.

Yet he has to continually honk his horn as the crazy flow of intertwining traffic, cars and many motorbikes, starts to flow on the streets again. And he has to pay extra attention to swerve around cattle lying in the middle of the few wide roads. Perhaps they have always done this or maybe now - with animal's sixth sense - have decided, with the residents of Kathmandu's skill at avoiding a collision with another vehicle or knocking someone down yards in front of them, or squashing a mad midday street dog, this place is the safer option than the threat of tumbling buildings.

Shops are open and trading, people engage in light hearted banter, laugh again. Nothing will stop these amazing people in getting back on their feet, walking on, heavy burdens on their backs through a storm. I feel hope, heart lifting.

Then Lalit turns round and warns us we're being kept away from the main areas of earthquake destruction, mainly over to the left in the centre, the Thamel district, the tight old maze of streets I'd wandered lost amongst, just…was it only 7 days ago? And historical places like Durbar Square. It's weird, like pockets of the city have been destroyed whilst other areas are relatively unscathed. Guess it's the old buildings or poorly constructed new ones that have been shaken to pieces?

I hope - after people are given the aid to be able to live a life again - that the money is raised to try and reconstruct the jewels in Kathmandu's (and those in other areas and towns) ancient crown in some way. Like the Everest industry, the country will badly need to be open for tourism business when the dust has settled, the tremors stop and lives have been rebuilt.

We're driven into the green oasis of the 4 star Park Village Hotel. The sun is shining, the temperature warm, even hot in direct sunlight. We're met by a New Zealand Intrepid rep, warm smile, who gives us a briefing: the hotel is intact but has sustained damage to several areas in the upper floors. With the constant threat of aftershocks it is best for us to sleep in the grounds, a few tents may become available, but our likely living quarters, for as along as it takes to organise flights home, is under the recess shelter (about 50ft long by 15ft deep) of a building that resembles an extra large bus shelter in a northern England town. Hot showers are available near the gym. None of us complain or have any inclination to.

Several of our group, however, have already organised flights home that evening, Irish Tom, Southern Paul, Lauren, Steph, Annabelle and Chandler. Whereas I, again with no smartphone or emergency funds, will have to wait; I wasn't due to fly home until May 7th, so could be stuck here for several days. If this is the case I would like to help the aid effort in some way, but this falls on deaf ears when mentioned to the Intrepid reps, they want to keep us safe here until we're flown out. Mel makes me feel better by saying I would be just another mouth to feed and potentially in the way if I don't have the necessary training and experience.

So we all gather for lunch on chairs around tables in a courtyard in front of the rear of the hotel, it will be our last supper as the united survivors of the Nepal earthquake 2015. Again the two Englishmen, Irishman and Scotsman have beers, San Miguel, to wash down the further luxury of chicken curries. We sit there in front of a grand hotel, surrounded by lush parkland, exotic birds with colourful long tail feathers and singing a tropical island song, to the right is a swimming pool, a beautiful bikini clad woman climbs out, water dripping off her tanned body, she goes to lie on a sun lounger by a man already stretched out on one soaking in the afternoon sun, waiters in smart attire come out and ask us if there's anything more we want.

I could be with friends in a luxury holiday resort, the hotel parkland is so big and filled with and bordered by such rich foliage and trees (and a high wall) that you can't see what city lies beyond. But out there is Kathmandu, on its knees. Far too many bodies lie in lines waiting to be cremated by the river or dug out of rubble, people possibly still trapped alive, surviving on any morsel of food that luckily could be within finger tip reach, or on droplets of water. Lives as shattered as their homes and businesses.

So it feels so wrong to be sat in the hotel scenario described, full bellies, a few last laughs, clinking glasses to toast a bond of lasting friendship and safe journeys home. I mention this to Scot's Dave, he puts another perspective in my mind, that Kathmandu needs foreigners to still come and stay in this style of hotel, spend money in the streets, go visit other areas of Nepal. Guess this is so, in time, but now? I'm not sure and feel guilty.

*

Aussie Paul is off to be reunited with his wife and sister up at Kopan Monastery and kindly asks if I'd like to go along with him to visit the holy sanctuary, if there is no chance of a flight home for me that night. There isn't so I jump at the chance, it was on my Kathmandu 'must-see' list anyway.

I ask Scot's Dave if he would like to come along too, he agrees and Hard Easy Rider Dave overhears and sort of invites himself. I don't begrudge him this of course, I'm just nervous of his loud hyped up presence up there and try to explain subtly that Kopan Monastery is a peaceful and deeply religious spot, quiet respect is the order of the day within its walls.

Before the taxi arrives we say goodbye to Irish Tom, Southern Paul, Steph, Lauren, Chandler and Annabelle. Hugs and handshakes all round, a sad parting of the ways for people who have shared an experience that will revisit all for the rest of our days and probably in the last hour before we shuffle off this mortal coil. If we are lucky enough to survive to a ripe old age and gently start to slip away with recall of our life and times. It's by no means certain to be afforded that privilege I'm beginning to realise.

The four of us heading for Kopan Monastery climb into the taxi and within minutes are back out of luxury into the rubble strewn streets of Kathmandu. Hard Easy Rider Dave has a window seat, winds the glass down, chocking smog quickly seeps in on this warm hazy evening, all his focus and that of his camera is on quake scenes we're soon encountering. He pulls the multi-snap trigger of his fairly expensive camera like he's back in his marine days firing an automatic rifle whilst running through ruined buildings in a war zone.

Rat-tat-tat-tat-tat.

'Oh wow, godda ged that, got it yeah, oh man and that!'

Rat-tat-tat-tat-tat.

Again you have to understand his heart is in the right place, he wants people to see the damage, it's just he lacks a little decorum and like Aussie Paul says: 'He verbalises every thought before it's gone through a thoughtful processing filter.' Maybe this is more an honest way to be, though?

The taxi driver negotiates his vehicle through poor back streets for a while, a shock to the eyes of privileged westerners on most normal Kathmandu days. Now with the effects of the earthquake evidently everywhere, my heart is as broken as much as the buildings, but not as much as those who once lived in them.

As we rise up the hill towards the monastery we go through more affluent neighbourhoods but still fairly poor by western standards. Round another bend our taxi narrowly avoids a collision with another one coming the opposite way, our driver swerving through a deep pot hole and onto the very edge of a road with a steep drop back down the hill on the far side. However, I now have faith in Nepalese drivers and faith in fate to keep me keeping on or not as it seems fit, out of my hands.

Up ahead is a stunning vista - Kopan Monastery sits majestically on its wooded island hill and beyond this, on another, a spectacular looking temple rises. Soon we pass by the security gate check and enter into the former and I soon know I've arrived at a nirvana of Nepal's capital. The grand gompa is straight ahead, masonry white with colourful statues and carvings around the entrance. Above the door is a Dharmachakra, a golden wheel of Dharma flanked by two deer, animals considered to represent compassion and peacefulness.

To the left of the gompa a small group of youthful looking monks sit around a table on a veranda that offers stunning views looking down to Kathmandu and the hills beyond. In the distance the Boudhanath Stupa, the largest in Kathmandu, one of the largest in the World, is visible, cracked but standing defiant.

I ask if I can take the monk's picture (after Hard Easy Rider Dave already has), one shakes his head and says: 'No.' They all laugh as I respectfully back away.

'He's joking,' smiles Aussie Paul.

First - after a message is sent to Paul's wife, Kerry, and nun sister, Janne, that he has arrived - we take off our shoes and prepare to enter the gompa. In the entrance area are paintings of the four Dharma kings, considered the protectors of Tibet. Then we are nearly knocked over by swarms of tiny monks rushing out, some carry mugs, text books, blankets and cuddly toys, bundles of robed joy each as they pass us by with excited chatter, the evening lessons and prayers completed.

Inside we're met by a huge statue of Lama Tsong Khapa (1357-1419) - at the far end, looking serenely down at us - whose teachings on Mahayana Buddhism the monastery follows. At his side are Shakyamuni Buddha, with Maitreya Buddha. It's a beautiful and elaborately decorated holy place of prayers and learning. Scot's Dave and Hard Easy Rider Dave soon take their photos and leave, Paul has gone to meet his family. I have the place nearly to myself, just one elderly monk sits in a chair to the right of the altar, he himself a picture of serenity, not moving a muscle, looking in my direction but as if deep in meditation, is this the visiting Lama? I wonder, and bow a little before him, clasp my hands and whisper 'Namaste.'

Then gesture to my camera and quietly ask if I can take his picture. The monk doesn't bat an eyelid or move an inch. I shuffle forward a little, a middle-aged monk comes in sweeping up, so I wander over to him: 'Is that the Lama? And would he mind if I take his photo?'

'I shouldn't think so, not now he's wax,' replies the monk with smile.

I blink in the candle light, and realise now, yes he is a wax effigy (of one of the Lama's that founded Kopan Monastery).

As I leave the gompa and join the others and start to stroll up the hill to the gardens, a senior nun (white with what sounds like a German accent) comes dashing out and starts to usher the little monks up to the gardens too: 'Quickly everyone, another big earthquake is predicted between now and 8.00 pm.'

Calm and nerves start to shatter again.

Our taxi driver informs us he can't wait until 8.00 pm. So the dilemma: go back through a maze of narrow streets full of damaged unstable buildings with a threat of another earthquake to hit any moment, or is it yet another rumour? Paul's sister, Janne, tells us that although there has been many aftershocks, this is the first time a senior nun or monk has given a warning about a quake on the way, this gives the warning credibility in my mind.

Hard Easy Rider Dave and Scot's Dave decide they'll take the risk and return to the taxi with the driver. I would prefer to stay for a while, and I don't think my nerves can stand another go at running the quake gauntlet or playing quake roulette. Also I'd only had a glimpse of Kopan monastery and was already falling in love with the holy place. So when Paul asked if I would like to stay the night there, I reply I would, very much.

The other two drive off with my hopes of a safe journey back to the hotel, I turn and join the flow of monks and nuns and visiting guests going up the hill to the gardens. Wow, what a great choice that turned out to be. The gardens are heavenly: a near 360 degrees view over Kathmandu, a variety of trees, small rolling grass hills containing a circular garden (about 20ft in diameter) with mini statues of Buddhist faith, plants and flowers and snippets of prayers and wise sayings of Buddha and the Dalai Lama. Two fantastic stupas (about 30ft high) elaborately decorated, in gold and bright colours; one has a 1000 mini Buddhas placed within it. Small trees sit on the well manicured lawns each draped with different coloured lights, one all red, one pink, one blue.

The mini monks cluster together for safety under a small palm tree on a little hill, they're quite calm, even playful. Paul's wife Kerry tells me that when the major quake struck they were all running around scared until the visiting Lama gathered them together to deliver soothing words, they've been under his peaceful influence ever since, staying calm during all the aftershocks including the big one of April 26th. I join other western guests that choose to sit near them, a feeling of happiness (you can't but have a big smile on your face in their presence), safety and serenity seeps into my soul.

A little while later I wander over to where Paul, Kerry and nun sister Janne are gathered. They're talking to a wise looking elderly monk and quickly I gauge, from their reverence and his aura, that this is the Lama. I immediately remove my hands from my pockets and clasp them together in front of me. Indeed he is the Lama and is introduced to me. He takes my hands within his and smiles.

'Namaste,' I say quietly.

'Ah, you see Everest on trek?' he asks with a warm smile.

'Er, no.'

'Don't worry, Everest will always be there, maybe next time you see her, when you come back,' he says and gives a little laugh.

'This,' I nod to the gardens and buildings, 'is more wonderful, I love it,' I say spontaneously.

The Lama smiles.

'Good answer,' comments nun Janne.

I'd had the privilege of meeting Lama Zopa Rimpoche, one of the founders of Kopan Monastery.

Once the home of the astrologer to the King of Nepal, Kopan is a now a thriving monastery of over 300 monks, and a spiritual oasis for hundreds of visitors yearly from around the world. Tibetan monks, who fled the persecution of the Chinese, arrived here in the 1950's and 60's. I'm told the story of a group of them being pursued by Maoist soldiers over the mountains, the likelihood of being shot if caught. But not being able to outrun them any more they sat down to pray; shortly afterwards a mist descended hiding them from the soldiers who passed them on by. The monks made it safely down to India and eventually Nepal and Kathmandu.

I briefly go with Paul and Kerry to their room for a welcoming cup of tea and biscuits and catch up chat. I feel a bit intrusive being here when the Australian couple are being re-united after the major earthquake separation, unsure of each other's fate for a while; it must have seemed an eternity. And I feel even more like I'm invading their privacy when it transpires I'll be sleeping on the floor of their bedroom. I was hoping there'd be a separate room to rest my weary head for the night. Kerry jokes that there was the chance of sharing a room with some nuns but it might have been looked on as inappropriate.

Talk returns to serious matters, when we join back with the others outside and I go with Janne to walk over to the canteen to help bring back food for people. She tells me about the moment the earthquake struck on April 25th. 'The dogs down in the streets below starting going crazy, barking and howls, minutes later everything began to violently shake and sway, a few moments of silence, then a surround sound of screams and shouts as pillars of dust clouds began to rise up from collapsed buildings.'

Janne pauses by an old brick building, built down the side of the sloping path back up to the gardens, and points it out to me, half the front is collapsed. 'Visitors accommodation, luckily it's old and was about to be refurbished so no one was staying there at the time, and one of the original meditation halls back over that way looks beyond repair, we were lucky, or blessed, but everyone has camped out in the grounds for safety ever since.'

Then it's like I go from a stark reminder of a nightmare into a fairytale bubble, a vision and sound bewitchingly beautiful and hypnotic: the gardens are now fully illuminated, the red, pink and blue trees glowing (regressing me back to one of my favourite and magical childhood memories of walking through the illuminated gardens of Torbay when on a holiday with my family). The stupas are lit up and a gentle light rests on the face of the gentle Lama. He's sat under a tree, gathered around him, sat on grass, are monks old and young (apart from the mini ones it being past their bedtime), as he leads them through a service of prayers, chants and mantras in memory of those killed, injured, missing or in need of assistance after the earthquake.

I'm both hypnotised and spiritualised: healing lullabies, the stars twinkle above, the moon beams, flowing prayers of love and hope that drift off down over the hill from Kopan, like a holy waterfall, down to Kathmandu. There, millions of lights are back on and shining out after days of power cuts, save for black holes in the suburbs, centres of life's extinguished, yet down below in Kathmandu a million lights that will never go out, shine on, souls reborn, rise up in a dream sequence moment.

One of the most uplifting, healing, beautiful and magical moments of my life. It's times like these you learn to love again, it's times like these you learn to live again. The nirvana illusion is only temporarily shattered by noticing the teenage monk in front of me, sat on the fringes, switching from reading prayers on a kindle (he probably knew them off by heart anyway) to exchanging messages on his smartphone (most of the monks and nuns seem to have them).

Paul and Kerry return, see I'm entranced and say it's ok for me to stay a while, they'll go put together my make-shift bed and come and fetch me a little later. I would love to sleep out here amongst the monks, under the stars and by the illuminated stupas and colourful singing ringing trees, but I don't have a tent and the resident mosquitoes would have a right royal feast on me, as is their right to do here, without me having the audacity to swat them, definitely not squash the bloody things, the devout Buddhists won't harm any living thing.

Feeling serene and calm for the first time since before the major earthquake, apart from the brief vision of the white winter hymnal night Christmas card scene in Namche, I drift away to bed with the sweet Buddha lullabies fading way into the night behind me.

If I had had one of those tents in the open ground I might have at last slept safe, sound and long for the first time since the trek began. But back in the confines of a partly damaged room - a crack runs along the wall above Kerry's bed - trying to sleep under an easy to shatter large window, beyond which is a long drop down into a valley and Kathmandu, my nerves begin to become on edge again.

And again I don't know if it's psychological, my shell-shocked psyche playing tricks, but the room seems to slightly rock constantly, then a little tremor? Huge disaster relief planes roar low over the top of Kopan Monastery (being so high up and standing out it appears it's used as a navigational marker by aircraft leaving Kathmandu airport as they sweep over and curve out into the countryside). Then the potential, animal world, earthquake alarm call keeps going off - a mass of dog barks and howls rise and fall from the streets below. The words of Janne on hearing them moments before the earthquake struck come back to haunt me, the night's rumour of another big quake, Paul snores on. I put my iPod phones in my ears, it does the trick, for half an hour or so I drift off to music.

Around 4.00 am, though, there is no doubt another aftershock occurs, this is more of a short sharp judder - the room definitely sways a little - than a tremor. Very quickly it's over with, but now I lie awake wishing the darkness before dawn away.

Fri May 1st 2015, Kathmandu, Nepal:

The moment the sun shines forth her new day light of hope - and it's May, my jinx month has passed - I quickly, but quietly, pull on my clothes and slip out of the room. On my iPod is the uplifting, in love with life, old reggae track 'Morning Sun' by Al Bary and the Cimarons. I quickly remove my iPod, though, to enjoy the tranquillity as I wander up to the gardens, tip-toeing by the tents where the Lama and the monks are still having sweet Buddha dreams. I come to a small gap in a wall that leads to a spiralling set of ascending steps to the very top of the hill, I go on up there. From a cluster of trees a cuckoo and other more exotic sounding birds, plus the usually cheeky crows, try to out do each other with the dawn chorus.

I reach a small grass plateau, more tents are scattered here, I circle around them clockwise thinking this is the correct direction to pass around sleeping monks as it is with stupas and shrines. At this high vantage point the view is spectacular, the sun rises above that big temple on the nearby hill, a new dawn for Kathmandu, bathed in a golden light that blurs out the damage, but not from memory, yet it all looks and feels so beautiful up here.

Back down in the gardens I come across a little group of western early bird humans, staying at the monastery, sat on benches. One, with an amiable face, big white beard and friendly manner makes me think of Santa Claus having a post Christmas vacation in another kind of magical grotto. We chat a while before I wander back up the hill towards our accommodation block. Along a passage running down the edge of this I come across an old meditation hall, abandoned and unused since being badly damaged in the earthquake.

There are warning signs on the door saying not to enter, but it's early morning, no one is around, the door is ajar, compelling the curious cat (who has already nearly used up 9 lives) to peer inside, then enter on in and gingerly have a look around. It's as it was left at the moment the earthquake struck and monks fled. Curved rainbow sunbeams shine in through broken windowpanes, colourful masonry - decorated with square patterns - fallen from cracked walls, lies all over the floor, silver prayer cups are scattered down there too, vases of flowers tipped over, the broken glass in the framed picture of the Dalai Lama, smiling out. A hard hitting lesson in Buddha's first noble truth. It's all quite eerie and reminds me of those photos showing the abandoned buildings of Chernobyl.

I return to the accommodation block, Paul and Kerry are nearly ready for us to go to breakfast. In the dining room a huge vat of porridge is on offer, sweetened with home made peanut butter, if you wish, toast and marmalade, mugs of tea and an extra treat, a monk brings us slices of mango.

I sit next to another western nun, Canadian, middle aged, shaven headed and robed. We chat, mostly about the earthquake and aftermath. I sit rapt, lump in my throat, pausing from eating my breakfast, as she tells me of going down into the streets to help in the rescue effort. I've a feeling she's holding back on the horrors she encountered, her eyes moist and haunted at telling me of finding children's shoes and other items of clothing amongst the rubble. I ask about the fate of a few locations I'd visited. Swayambhunath, 'the monkey temple' was badly damaged she informs me, people buried, the heart strings pulling image of the beggar children on the steps immediately flashes into my minds eye. She's heard of monkeys there seen limping along with a broken arm.*

90

*Several weeks after arriving home, footage and news of the devastation of this temple will again affect me deeply, send me spiralling into depression. The hard hitting fact - that's where I was just 3 days before, at the time the big quake struck. I'd loved it there that sunny day, one of my favourite memories of Kathmandu before April 25th 2015.

The see-sawing of emotions continues, sadness then spiritual healing, hopelessness then hope, heart broken then melted, soul full of sink holes then soaring. All the positives here come to the fore on leaving the canteen and encountering the endearing energy of the mini monks: risen from their slumber, they're sat in two rows on mats, under a open fronted shelter (that has Buddhist icons in glass cases at the rear), some have slept there. They're singing morning prayers whilst having their breakfast - mugs of tea and on top of these, whilst still hot, they place bread buns to soften them up.

It's the most wonderful music to the ears, totally enchanting and soul elevating. Maybe this is ignorance on my part but to me it resembles the unforgettable African village songs at the start of the film *Zulu*. On it goes, drifting up into the golden morning air, spreading happiness, hope, love and faith. It rises and falls as some naughty lads try to out sing others, guess this competitive edge helps them learn the prayers off by heart?

To accompany this mesmeric melody, older monks in the gompa, 30 yards away, begin chanting mantras. The spiritual sounds mingle and blend perfectly, the dawn chorus of the birds in the trees the backing choir.

The mini monks are lucky: selected from poor backgrounds they're given a great start in life, in terms of schooling and spirituality. When they come of age it's up to them if they want to continue as a devoted Buddhist monk or leave to pursue another life with perfect grounding to set them on their way. And they learn the value of true friendship too; you'll see them walking hand in hand with their best friend around the grounds.

I'm also unexpectedly gifted with the endorphin release of laughter for a few brief moments of escapism. A western youth, staying at the monastery, comes walking down the steps near the drive up to the gompa. Lying in the sun are two scruffy street dogs, who have had the cheek to find their way into the monastery grounds and now know the monks will tolerate and probably feed them. One raises its head slightly to watch the youth walk towards it. In reply the youth starts waving at the dogs, far too animatedly, as when he gets within a few feet of passing them the dogs spring up and chase him off into a shop, barking frustratedly at being disturbed, then wander back to their original spot and crash down again to sunbathe.

Monks are busy loading a lorry full of earthquake aid items, ready to again set out and help in the rescue and relief efforts of shattered communities of Nepal.

Then it's time to leave this sanctuary, its healing effects still coursing through veins, into my psyche, heart and soul. Even though I've only slept about an hour or so in the last frantic 24 hours, I feel no fatigue at this stage after the positive effects of monastery. The new tales of sorrow I've heard, and the ruined meditation hall, are all there swirling around the back of my mind in the dark whirlpool of earthquake experiences, but for now a buoyant Buddhist built boat is keeping me afloat in calmer, luminescent seas.

One personality gift I've been blessed with is being able to see beauty all around me when it passes others by (hence staring out of the window of the train to London when others could only see false pixel images mentioned earlier), mainly nature. Stood outside the monastery gates with Paul and Kerry, waiting for our taxi, at the top of a fairly poor street that rises up the hill, I see a little oasis. Guess it would be just the overgrown unkempt garden of a council house back home, 10ft down a wall in front of an old rickety house, are wildflowers. Standing tall, proud and beautiful above the rest are a group of giant red lilies, butterflies flutter around them, a movement in the bushes - that grow on top of the wall - and I spot a lizard, about 5 inches long, sandy coloured body and deep orange head, pausing to check me out before scurrying off. I do jump a little when just above my hand - that's resting on a lamppost - is a huge fearsome looking black and red hornet. Before us is a more familiar sight, swarms of mayflies hover just as they will be doing back in my corner of English countryside.

Then there's the sound of a motorbike, a Nepalese youth on a pretty decent Suzuki swerves into view. Motorbikes are a must-have status symbol for Kathmandu youths, and the better the bike the better the girl you can attract it seems, his passenger is a stunner, she grips his waist tight, sunshine smile on her face. Kathmandu stretches away into the distance, again the undamaged huge stupa, Boudhanath, rising above the fractures, the eyes of Buddha unblinking in faith, the majestic hills beyond. Still in my temporary state of nirvana, all these tiny elements of Nepal fill me with hope for the country's rebirth this spring morning.

Then one of those huge cargo planes, here delivering essential earthquake aid, soars overhead with a deafening roar. And our taxi arrives to take me away from this paradise island up in the clouds. We have to face reality, sink back down into Kathmandu, and I'll start to drown again.

The trouble with my 'gift' it has the dark flipside, throw in hypersensitivity and getting too emotional over things at times, and I'll also spot or hear things (in normal everyday life, even the coldest of hearts would melt with emotion in a disaster zone such as Nepal) so sad or moving that it breaks my heart and can even reduce me to tears, little things at times, that no one else notices. In this earth shattering, people slaying, environment I'm soon starting to dissolve inwardly again.

This taxi driver goes a different way back from the one who brought us here; tighter, poor streets. We turn down one and can travel no further along that road, a bus, tossed into a ditch by the earthquake, crumpled at the front, its rear end sticking up into the air at a 45 degree angle, is at that moment being secured with chains in an attempt to drag it back out. So we have to take a further detour, past more families living on wasteland, in tents, under tarpaulin, bonfires lit, cooking food, buckets of water.

We pass down the end of one street and the taxi driver points out of the window to a pile of rubble and timbers at the far end: 'That was church, it collapse and kill eighty people.'*
*Saturday, the day of the earthquake, is the day of worship in Nepal, so the church was full.

Further along he points over roof tops. 'Over that way is a building so damaged and in a dangerous state that nobody dare enter, it could be weeks, months, before bodies are recovered.'

We arrive back at oasis drive, the entrance to Parkland Village Hotel, where I'm dropped off and say sad goodbyes to Paul, a truly great, humble, caring and level-headed person who I quickly came to like, very much. And his wife Kerry, only known a day but made me feel so welcome.

I begin to traipse down the drive but security stop me, I'm beginning to look and smell like a tramp now, I don't care. I explain I'm with Intrepid, my name is asked, a phone call made and eventually I'm let in. I'm lifted in finding that Scot's Dave, Hard Easy Rider Dave and Dr Mel are still here. Then an added bonus, Moh and Gae turn up; we all assumed they'd flown straight out, but they'd been put up in a nearby hotel. Scot's Dave is particularly happy to see Moh and they spend a few more precious moments together, wandering off. Dave has managed to secure himself a tent further into the parkland, separated a little way from the rest, crafty devil.

We have a meal together, Hard Easy Rider Dave is buzzing as usual, Gae, shy and sweet as usual, and Dr Mel upbeat, resolute and practical as usual; it's her unbreakable character traits I gain strength from at this time. Then she too is away, off to meet up with friends somewhere else in Kathmandu, before going off to put her medical skills to valuable use in the earthquake zone.

Just as Mel leaves Lalit turns up, and we have an invite, to his home, he only lives just up the hill it turns outs. Hard Easy Rider Dave, Gae and me follow him on up there. His house is one of the grandest in a decent neighbourhood. A gleaming white 4 storey tower, edged with colourful decoration, a testament to his achievements and hard work in life: starting out as a guide, on to teaching climbing in Norway, a time in London I believe, to becoming top trek leader on both sides of the Himalayas, Nepal and Tibet. Yet on closer inspection, as he shows us around, his family dream palace he has so long grafted for is in danger of tumbling down, cracks are everywhere in the only recently completed home. It may stay upright in the near future but a structural engineer may deem it too unsound to live in and order it demolished.

Our hearts go out to this valiant and noble man who led us on a dream trek then out of a nightmare. He's 45 now, you need to be physically very fit for what he does, time is running out if he has to start again.

We're introduced to his family - wife, teenage son and daughter - and taken up to their living room on the top floor, given food, tea, hospitality and friendship. The view from out on the flat roof terrace is wonderful, over large areas of Kathmandu down the hill; I see Kopan Monastery and the temple beyond. Towards the north-west the valley hills rise.

'Further over that way whole suburbs have been destroyed, many killed,' says Lalit sadly.

Hanging above the roof terrace is a concrete water tank held up by two pillars, one of which is badly cracked; one more strong aftershock and it could topple over into the streets below. We can only hope his life and home can be patched up, this man deserves that at the very least.

'If you need a meal and hotel too expensive you come here for one,' he tells us.

We return to the hotel, Gae links back up with Moh, and they're shortly to share a taxi to the airport with Scot's Dave. More hugs and very sad partings, and I watch them drive away. Then I remember Rahul, and can't recall the last time I saw him, but he's disappeared again, or evaporated into the clouds and fallen back down into India like early monsoon rain.

That just leaves Hard Easy Rider Dave and me, I could do with his turbo charged energy at this time for sure, but even he's sitting still at this moment. After smoking his backy he puts African rap on, no doubt, lies back on his mat, and even closes his eyes. He does want me to stick around and 'hey dude wanna go see some quake damage.' All in a good cause maybe (although everyone will have seen more shocking footage on the 24 hour news channels back home that hopefully will give them cause to donate to the disaster fund) but I can't spend days being a voyeur to people's misery if there isn't anything I can do to help, just getting in the way, I'd feel more like a griffon vulture circling.

Like the rest I now need to go home, and they've all gone. Without their friendship and shared moral support all the ghastly experiences, the lack of sleep, shell shock, and loneliness, overwhelms me and I hate myself for allowing it to and any hint of self pity that tries to creep in.

I go along a narrow walkway to sit by a little round water feature on my own. Usually the sound of trickling water would calm me, but today it feels like Chinese water torture. The sun beats down, an oppressive heat, I feel like a scruffy, half crazy street dog that's wandered into this exclusive area of luxury parkland but no one dare chase me off fearing I might be rabid. To go jump into that swimming pool fully clothed - water bombing the sunbathers - would be heaven, but I deny thoughts of enjoying myself, I don't even go for a free shower, I can wait until I'm off this soil where people are without easy access to water.

I finally see the Intrepid rep around again and inform him that Scot's Dave had checked the web for me and that there are flights out to Manchester that evening, could he arrange to get me on one? I think he can see I'm breaking down. On seats in the plush hotel foyer I watch him make a series of smiley business to business etiquette Skype calls, and an hour later he has secured it with Qatar airlines to get me on a flight out of Kathmandu at 8.30 pm, arriving in Manchester at 1.00 pm the next day.

At 6.00 pm that night I say my goodbyes to Hard Easy Rider Dave, who seems surprised and disappointed I'm leaving. 'You're some character, good luck on the Camino,' I say.

'I'm having t-shirts done next dude - Quake Survivor - with the Camino trail on the top, Buddha eyes and the appeal.'

'Great, I'll look out for it.'

I share a taxi to the airport with an Irish guy who's been in another Intrepid Base Camp group. I have to wind the window up as we trundle and swerve through the streets, in the warm humid air the choking pollution grabs you by the back of the throat, the driver wears a mask. More people line the side of the roads, gather on grass verges and wastelands, seemingly getting on with their lives, but it's hard to differentiate those who were living in third world poverty before the earthquake and those who are now homeless and destitute because of it. There are smiles and stoicism amongst them, but you wonder of their fate when the monsoon rains come or god forbid another big quake hits. Guess in the city they can find shelter from the rain, it will be a lot harder for those in the wasted villages down in the northern valleys near the epicentre.

The check-in for the airlines was orderly and fast enough to get through, then into the big departure hall. Many a weary, bewildered, tired and haunted face are gathered here, slumped on seats. A group of men wearing blue uniforms with union jacks on badges are stood nearby: a UK international search and rescue team. One tells me they've been out in the devastated areas north of Kathmandu. I don't press them on what they've seen, just shake his hand. He points out another group of British men sat side by side on a row of seats: soldiers, who were preparing for an attempt to summit Everest. They had a lucky escape from the avalanche, several were picked up and carried along by it; one has his head bandaged. There's that 1000 yard stare on a few faces.

Outside the window on the runway another of those huge Russian cargo planes rolls to a stop. Other countries like China use these planes but this one had the lettering and badge of Russia itself. I've seen more of them than cargo planes from other countries, you only hear the negatives of Russia on the UK and American news I'm thinking. A Qatar airliner soon comes into view too, my flight out is announced on the tannoy. Everyone rushes forward to the boarding gate. The British soldiers look on with disdain. 'Calm down, you're all getting on the same plane,' one shouts.

It's not long before we're all in our seats but it takes an age for the engines to fire up. As the time dragged I was probably not the only one praying that another huge aftershock didn't hit and cancel the flight. Soon I'll be lifted up and away from that, leaving the poor people of Nepal behind to cope with being aftershock psychological punch bags - you think you ever get used to aftershocks (after being in a major earthquake) even the small ones? You DON'T, at the first tremble you're gripped with fear, anxiously waiting to see if the tremor grows in strength - on top of the death and destruction aftermath of the big quake.

There's a collective sigh of relief as the plane finally soars into the air. It's night-time and the orange light sprinkled blackness down there could be any country. It's quiet in the cabin, people sleep or watch something on the interactive screen on the seat backs. To pass time and take my mind off things I watch a collection of old Premier League goals for a while: United in their 90's prime, opening up a happy chapter in my autobiography, *If the Kids are United*. I think of Phurba Sherpa and his Manchester United loving team, hoping they can be united in happier times again soon, worries aside, the Lukla pitch cleared of tents as families return to their rebuilt homes, the lads free and happy to look forward to a game of football on Sundays.

Pretty stewardesses bring food and drink around. Then I try to grab a little sleep but just stare like a zombie instead; I listen to my iPod, until the plane touches down in Doha and a spontaneous ripple of applause breaks out.

It's 1.20 am here, my connecting flight to Manchester isn't until 7.00 am. Luckily Scot's Dave had told me that if you have to wait over 4 hours for a connection they have to put you up in a hotel. This is confirmed at the arrivals desk; me, two other bearded weary looking Nepal trekkers and an Asian guy are to be put up in a hotel in Doha City for the night. We have to wait on some seats for a rep to come and issue us with room tickets. By the time we're getting in a taxi it's getting on for 2.00 am (one thing I do notice is the oppressive heat, even at this time of the early hours, and this is where they're going to play the football World Cup in the daytime!)

We travel for 20 minutes along a modern motorway, through land reclaimed from the desert, now filled with a few industrial units and hotels, a large mosque, all surrounded by palm trees and areas of landscaped green oasis. Then we arrive in the outskirts of Doha City and pull up at a luxury hotel; a man opens the doors for us. Inside a huge shimmering chandelier hangs in the foyer. The man behind the desk looks with disdain at the 3 scruffy travellers dumped on them, and directs us to some leather seats. Lift doors open, a man with shoulder length silver hair and an English accent steps out; a gold watch on his wrist, the waft of expensive aftershave as he passes by with a group of Arab men. Two attractive women, short skirts and bling, arrive back at the hotel, whilst we sleepily wait for the keys to our room.

It's without doubt the most luxurious hotel room I've ever been in, but it's 2.30 am now, I've just time to look out of the window at the glowing skyscrapers of this rich city. This place would have been a poor third world country too without oil revenue, I'm thinking; before climbing into the most comfortably bed I've ever lay my head down in. I could sleep for a week in it, I'm out for the count as soon as my head touches the pillow, but the count seems like 1 second as the 5.00 am alarm call I asked for jars me awake. I do have time to afford myself with one genuine luxury, the power shower, it's the best one I've had since the one at Butlins in Minehead after spending 5 days without one at the scorching sun kissed Glastonbury Festival 2010. I leave the beard, not for some Himalayan badge of honour; I've become quite accustomed to it and feel like I would be scraping Nepal away from me if I shaved.

The following are my photos of the aftermath of the Nepal Earthquake, April 25th 2015 – Namche Bazaar, Lukla, the return to Kathmandu and the visit to Kopan Monastery.

Kopan Monastery

Saturday May 2nd, Doha to Manchester:

The Asian guy, who'd travelled from the airport with us, is catching the same taxi back as me too. We were all too tired to chat in the early hours, but now we strike up conversation. He's actually Nepalese, who left the country to work abroad but is now returning there and to his family at the hour of need. He's taking a tent as they're in short supply over there and a few essential items. Then on the journey back to the airport he talks about his love of the English Premiership; football always a way to bond with people in my travel through life, in every circumstance. I shake his hand and wish him and his family well and a safe passage in returning to them, and feel sad as I stand and watch him check the flight time to Kathmandu on the big board and walk on with his head held high.

I go for breakfast at Burger King, and have a Steakhouse sandwich, fries and a coke. I'm sat at the exact same table - with the view to the shimmering towers of Doha City - as I was on the morning of April 21st, when excitedly looking forward to arriving in Kathmandu, seeing its ancient temples and squares before setting off to Everest. It feels so weird to be back here, like I fell asleep at the table and some giant hand plucked me up and dropped me down into a wonderfully crazy, golden lit, hazy dream or film that mutated into a nightmare or had an unexpected dark twist in the plot. I go through the photos on my camera to confirm it was real, and deciphering my scrawled handwriting in my notepad (light-hearted and uplifting until the events of April 25th) really hammers it home. I was in a major earthquake, a disaster zone.

I was hoping to get a bit more kip on the long 7 hour flight to Manchester, and do occasionally nod off, drool running down onto my beard as I jump awake, when someone passing down the aisle I'm leaning into, catches my arm and I think a tremor is going off. I'm sat on the right seat of 4 in the centre of plane. A couple were in the ones to my left, the woman in the seat next to me, but when I come around I notice they've hutched along to the far end, away from the drooling tramp, and realise I still smell too (after the shower I still threw back on my hiking gear and boots not wanting to try and squash them into my over-packed chaotic rucksack with the clocking ticking down to my taxi).

On the flight are tanned people travelling back from holidays in the likes of Australia, exciting chatter goes on around me. I try and watch the film *Birdman*, but half asleep, finding it hard to focus, I couldn't tell you what happened, other than a big crazy bird that turned into a vulture in my drowsy dream state. For hours I stare at the interactive flight map on the screen, wishing the little animated plane would move faster over the landscape of southern Europe, I even try to push it along with my finger.

I hear a Lancashire voice behind me say: 'It's only bloody six degrees in Manchester and raining.'

Originally - on setting off on the trip - I was hoping a glorious spring would turn into an early summer on my return. But as the plane touches down on home soil and I look out at leaden slate grey Manchester skies, feel the cold and see the rain fall, I don't mind at all, this is England, home; I love it and feel lucky to have been born here. Even with its maddening politicians (I'm now going to have to endure in the run up to a General Election I should have missed), rules and regulations, red tape, nonsense nanny state and self centred world importance and ignorance, obsession with celebrity and royalty.

It's the latter and not politicians I have to endure when I arrive back at my sister Elaine's and put on the TV for any latest news on the Nepal earthquake. There's not a chance of the human disaster in a foreign land getting 5 minutes of coverage this day, all other news is pushed aside, for today a new royal baby has been born - a daughter for Wills and Kate - into privilege. Cameras stay focused on the door to the maternity unit for hours with the asinine comments from the royal correspondent: 'I can confirm the Queen is wearing pink today….just heard that a BBC microphone has been savaged by a security dog.'

After being fed by Elaine, and a catch up chat, a shower and putting on the only items of clean clothing I've managed to dig out my rucksack, a decent night's sleep (even if it is only on a settee), I turn to the previous week's newspaper coverage of the Nepal earthquake (that Elaine has saved for me), the internet and catch up TV to see footage, photos and read about the full wide scale of the disaster for the first time.

When I get back home to Nottinghamshire I discover I've been on the front page and featured in several regional newspapers (even miles away in the Yorkshire Evening Post). Basically they've lifted timeline messages from my Facebook page. That was over a week ago, yesterday's news and it appears so too is the Nepal earthquake on the BBC (SKY and ITV continue to do more in-depth special news reports to their credit). They're in full swing o meter General Election mode. General dismay from much of the north of Watford Gap as the Tories creep, slime and crawl into No.10.

'David Cameron will spend the weekend in Number 10 deciding on the make-up of his new cabinet,' BBC Breakfast.

I'd have thought Heath Ledger Joker make-up from *Batman* would be most apt. I look out of the window and I'm stared out from a large pair of evil looking eyes on a placard (on a lamppost at the end of the street) that sums up the kind of misanthropic malaise the Tories have created. 'We're Watching You!' it warns, this time about dog muck. But we're watched with mistrust in everything we do. When you see a pair of eyes on something in Nepal it means Big Buddha is looking out for you - peace, harmony and wisdom, when you see a pair of eyes on something in England it means Big Brother is out to get you, state control, paranoia.

Even when the second big earthquake hits Nepal on May 12th, causing more deaths, destruction and thousands more to live out in the open, the BBC is still so busy patting themselves on the back at being *the* political channel that they only give it five minutes on the 10.00 o'clock news and nothing at all on *Newsnight*.

A week later though they do at last give a considerable amount of time on breakfast news to the earthquake, a 4.1 one in Kent: 'It was ferocious, the bed shook, seagulls screamed.'

On May 12th my blood froze, when watching the breaking news on SKY, and it was revealed the epicentre was near Namche Bazaar. An anxious wait went on for hours: the strongly built western style guesthouses again largely withstood the new quake but parts of the old village were further damaged, including the schoolhouse; luckily the children were out in the playground at the time and no deaths were reported there.

I receive sadder news via Facebook, my Manchester United supporting friend Phurba Sherpa posts the following on his timeline:

'Nepal is very sad now. Nepali lost their not only home but also family members as well one of them Everest region, also today earthquake had affected very badly. I am so sad and me and my family all outside Another earthquake in Lukla. All house damaged. We are all sitting outside. My house also badly damaged.'

All I can think of to help is start an online funding campaign, 'Nepal United' using a picture of Phurba's team wearing Manchester United shirts and post it on the Stretford Ender Facebook group I run. Even though people not involved in the quake see it as yesterday's news (I noticed the buckets at checkout in a local supermarket now only had a few coins in them) I manage to raise my initial target of £1000 within a few days (mainly from the once notorious Red Army Stretford Enders of the 70's and 80's) to transfer to him. The only other thing I can do is give words of support. When he sends me another picture of his team in United shirts I tell him of the Busby Babes dying in the Munich air crash, Matt Busby seriously injured; and how the club rose up phoenix like from the ashes, Busby leading them to back to victory.

And he daily asks how I am.

Phurba, Nepal and its people are going to need a lot more support to get back on their feet. Shelter from the oncoming monsoon is needed immediately, as is clean running water, food and medical supplies. Then the long process of rebuilding homes, the psychological damage has to be addressed, then piecing back together the shattered fragments of the Nepal's rich history in the likes of Durbar Square and the Swayambhunath Temple, landslides cleared, the Everest industry back attracting the climbers and trekkers of the world.

Despite experiencing many things I love about England, and the banging your head on the wall inducing annoyances, it's weeks before my head feels like it's truly landed back in the country. A couple of times I wake in the middle of the night and think I'm in a teahouse and another aftershock has shaken me awake.

Then one afternoon, when still feeling drained, I take advantage of the peace and quiet: the neighbours to my left have moved out and the one to my right is away, my living room is on the back, with no houses facing that way, the back garden drops away to a recreation ground and nature trail, wooded hills beyond. On the branches of two trees in my garden, visible out of the window, I've draped prayer flags I bought in Lukla, more hang from a shelving unit in my living room, above a postcard of the Kumari, candles, a mini prayer wheel (that I spin every day) and a colourful Buddha Mandala calendar page (that was used to wrap the prayer wheel in by the shopkeeper). A corner of a foreign land forever has an English soul and a small corner of my living room and garden forever Nepal.

I take a nap this quiet afternoon - a dog barking on the park wakes me. Still half asleep I see the personal memorial Nepal souvenirs, the prayer flags flapping in the breeze, raindrops run down the window like tears, above the horizon rises a mountainous conical shaped cloud. In this brief moment I think I'm in Nepal and seeing Everest at last, just a very brief dreamy moment, but seconds later as the illusion drifts away, I know I have to return to Nepal, in memory and to encounter the mountain that captivates and captures man's soul.

You may be reading this in 2016 or when the earthquake of April 25th 2015 is in recent memory, or 1, 2, 5 years on and Nepal is still healing and rebuilding. You may be reading this 10, 50 or 100 years or more in the future from these words and hopefully there's not been another major earthquake, the country is stable and thriving in all aspects of its being. You may believe in the Buddhist philosophy of the human condition being just one lifetime in which, through the four noble truths, you can gain nirvana. You'll get enlightenment and shown the path to achieve this in Nepal. You may believe that earth is a one off jewel encrusted Gaia floating in a vast black sea, and you'll find some of her most precious jewels, in terms of landscape, in Nepal.

Epilogue

At the time of writing over 8800 people were killed in the 7.8 magnitude Nepal Earthquake (the energy release of which had the power of over 500 atomic bombs dropped on Hiroshima) of April 25th 2015, nearly 18,000 injured, over 500,000 homes destroyed or damaged, leaving millions of people homeless. A huge international aid and rescue effort began. Around 900 people were rescued from collapsed buildings, aid distributed to a near 1.5 million people. This is still going on with the monsoon season approaching.

22 people were killed and over 60 injured in the avalanches caused by the earthquake near Mount Everest.

Student, Matthew Carapiet, 23, from Kent, was one of two Britons to die in the earthquake, whilst trekking in the Langtang Valley; the other was an expat living in Hong Kong.

Kathmandu Valley dropped by about a metre and even Everest shrank by a few inches.

In the second 7.2 major earthquake on May 12th 2015 a further 218 died (this included 6 American Marines helping with the rescue and aid effort who were killed in a helicopter crash) and thousands more were injured, many more people were left homeless.

All of our group took the children of Nepal to our hearts, they were cute, funny, full of life and smiles; be it the mini monks of the monasteries, street kids or the ones we encountered on the trek. So one of the most sickening news stories to emerge after the earthquake was that of human traffickers, luring orphaned children, and those from vulnerable families, into prostitution and slavery.

60% of Nepal's heritage buildings were badly damaged or completely destroyed in the earthquake. This is the fate of those I visited or saw.

Durbar Square:
Maju Deval 'the hippie temple' – destroyed.

The old 11th century 'Kathmandu house' – destroyed. I don't know the fate of the holy man I was blessed by in there.

Trailokya Mohan Narayan temple, the tallest in the square, dedicated to Vishnu – destroyed.

The octagonal Krishna temple, built in 1649 – destroyed.

The King Pratap Malla column fell to the ground.

An outer wall housing the large war drums fell but can be repaired.

The nine-story Palace Basantapur tower lost its top two floors.

Although buildings crumbled all around it, the temple of the Kumari survived, safe inside the little living goddess was evacuated to an area outside of Kathmandu.

The stupa at the ancient Swayambhunath 'monkey temple' was damaged but stayed standing, many buildings surrounding it however collapsed, burying several people. Sacred monkeys were injured too.

From Swayambhunath I'd seen the gleaming white tower of Dharahara, 203ft high, this collapsed killing 180 people.

Much of the Thamel district surrounding the Kathmandu Guest House was badly damaged, many people died there.

Of the EBC group:
Many of us were re-united on Facebook. There was a sense of despondency at not having been able to have helped the people of Nepal more at the time. Several of us started fund raising campaigns or wired cash. Hard Easy Rider Dave set off on The Camino Way to raise funds for Nepal. Dr Mel was back doing exemplary medical care in the Kathmandu Valley.

There was also the collective difficulty at adjusting to life back home for a while. Aussie Paul found sanctuary back on his sheep farm, Southern Paul happiness at being reunited with his wife and 4 kids, Annabelle was re-united with her Swedish boyfriend, looking forward to university life in America, where her 'brother' Chandler had returned. Starting my own fund campaign, then friends, family and the beauty of spring in England - especially being the bluebell woods in D.H. Lawrence countryside, near where I live - and writing (again) was my healing process. The others drifted back into normal life, but changed forever.

Some found the best way of moving on was moving on and immediately travelled again. The last I heard of Irish Tom he was in Africa. Scot's Dave went to Indonesia, his guide was a certain 'Sunny' Moh.

Phurba Sherpa and Gyaljen Sherpa joined us on Facebook. First their posts tell of living in tents, on to photos being posted showing them uniting to rebuild Lukla school, getting their community back on their feet. Then Phurba tells me his team are off on a 2 day walk to play in a football tournament again, Lukla United.

All of us will never forget the events in Nepal, before and after the 25th of April 2015, count our blessings and value the gift of life, every day.

Printed in Great Britain
by Amazon.co.uk, Ltd.,
Marston Gate.